Robert Kanigel

# VINTAGE READING

## FROM PLATO
## TO BRADBURY

*A Personal Tour
of Some of the
World's Best Books*

**bancroft
press**

BALTIMORE, MD

Copyright 1998 by Robert Kanigel

Published by Bancroft Press
P.O. Box 65360, Baltimore, MD 21209   (800) 637-7377


ISBN 0-9631246-7-6
Library of Congress Catalog Card Number
Printed in the United States of America


First edition


1   3   5   7   9   10   8   6   4   2

Cover art © Barbara Kiwak, 1997
Designed by Melinda Russell, Bancroft Press
Distributed to the trade by National Book Network, Lanham, MD

*Also by Robert Kanigel*

APPRENTICE TO GENIUS:
The Making of a Scientific Dynasty

THE MAN WHO KNEW INFINITY:
A Life of the Genius Ramanujan

THE ONE BEST WAY:
Frederick Winslow Taylor and the Enigma of Efficiency

# Introduction

## ONE
## On Everyone's List of Literary Classics

## TWO
## On Many a List for Burning
### Heretics, Subversives, Demagogues

# THREE
## Books That Shaped the Western World

# FOUR
## Making Hard Work Easy
### The Great Popularizers

# NINE

## *The Realm of the Spirit*

### Holy and Human

# *Introduction*

Somehow, despite myself, I'd gotten stuck in the same stupid bind as everybody else. By the early 1980s, after more than a decade spent keyboard-pecking and deadline-squirming to the freelance writer's quickstep, I felt like every harried business executive, teacher, programmer, or parent—or, for that matter, like every drudge of a nine-to-fiver: I loved to read, yet wasn't reading much. And what I did read was usually what I had to read. Oh, one time an assignment to profile Yiddish storyteller Isaac Bashevis Singer gave me the chance to read some of his strange, otherworldly creations. And a piece about city living sent me back to Jane Jacobs' classic, *The Life and Death of Great American Cities*. But more often, I suffered the sad affliction of our age: Hopelessly caught up in the now, I had no time for those great old books of richness, subtlety, and originality I'd grown up hearing about, that were part of my cultural heritage, and that I really wanted to read.

As it happens, my writing included the occasional book review, usually of books editors assigned to me. But, the thought struck me one happy day, what if I picked what I'd review? And not books just then the object of some publicist's intemperate pleadings, but classics of their kind, ones that had been around for fifty years, maybe, or five hundred.

I approached an editor at the Baltimore *Sun*. Would he be interested in reviews of old books? No, not too often, I reassured him. Not so often as to compete for editorial space with the latest war, fashion, or scandal. But maybe, say, once a month?

Thus was born "Vintage Reading," a column which appeared first in the Baltimore *Sun*, then for much longer in the *Evening Sun* (now sadly folded into its bigger brother) and concurrently, for a while, in the *Los Angeles Times*, where it was called "ReReading." For seven years, I took

1

time out from articles on bicycle racing, laser surgery, and the space shuttle to dip into Kipling and Thucydides, Flaubert and William James.

"Vintage Reading" gave me the chance to read old books I wanted to read, then turn around and write about what reading them had been like. I am forever grateful for those years now. "Vintage Reading" was my own private liberal arts education (term papers and all). Except that rather than write to suit some professor's pedagogical agenda, I was writing for readers of a daily newspaper—folks like myself who, however intelligent and professionally accomplished they might be, rarely made time for books they didn't have to read.

My credentials? Those only of a working writer, and of a long-time voracious reader and lover of books. The essays you find here are not the work of a scholar or academician. They are the work, and the pleasure, of a species of literary dilettante. They are middle-brow essays reflecting, I suppose, middle-brow sensibilities. They draw their inspiration from the friendly, more or less knowledgeable guide who brings to life the ruins of Pompeii or the glories of Chartres for visiting tourists.

A tour guide will not, of course, suit everyone. In particular, those of more academic stripe may come away hungry from these brief essays. They are, first of all, brief. But more, that very delight and sense of wonder many of us felt in college, say, as we met new authors and new books—an experience we associate, after all, with eighteen-year-olds— may seem to more refined palates simplistic or naive. Still, I offer no apologies. My wish all along has been not to "protect" the great books behind daunting battlements, but to lower the drawbridge and invite readers inside.

Other readers may question my particular choices. Some, certainly, are predictable enough; who would omit Thomas Wolfe's *Look Homeward, Angel* or Gibbon's *Decline and Fall of the Roman Empire* from any list of candidates for rereading, or first reading? But other choices may seem problematical or perverse—such as works by the relatively unknown

English detective story writer R. Austin Freeman, the Bavarian fantasist Gustav Meyrink, or the now forgotten American novelist Joseph Hergesheimer; or by frank popularizers like C. R. Ceram; or distinctly unliterary figures like, well, Adolf Hitler.

The brutal truth, dear reader, is that I chose these books for my benefit, not yours—because I wanted to learn something; or venture to an old time, or new place; or because circumstances awakened me to the merits of some long-dead author; or in a few cases because a book just happened to cross my desk or catch my eye. Typically, my choices reflected the whim of the moment, so they include vintage books that might not make every top ten list of immortal classics, but to which I nonetheless turned for literary, emotional, or intellectual sustenance at the time.

Is this, I wonder, so wrong a way to direct one's reading? Maybe that seat-of-the-pants hunch about what to read next makes as much sense as leaving it to nagging shoulds-and-oughts. A friend gave me an old leather-bound copy of Longfellow's *Hiawatha*; it sat on a shelf for months until I was ready for it—and then, suddenly, I was. A book mentioned to me a hundred times might leave me unmoved; then, the 101st, I'd pounce upon it. That's how it was, for example, with *The Federalist Papers*.

From the beginning, I was determined to free my choices from chains of class and category. I wanted neither to flee from intellectually formidable territory nor dismiss lighter, more popular works just because they were popular; neither to exclude familiar names just because they were familiar, nor omit the unknown and idiosyncratic. Readers will find here mixed together not only fiction and nonfiction but an epic poem, a short story collection, a book from the Bible, even a reference work or two. I did, however, exclude plays; Shakespeare and Beckett are primarily theatrical experiences, not for reading. And this being *Vintage* Reading, I've included only books that have had time to age; readers will find here nothing more recent than the early 1960s.

I hope readers will bring to my attention favorites of their own they'd like me to know about. But I hope they will not introduce them to me as books I've unaccountably "left out"; I've left out *thousands*, many of which I hope to some day read. To me, it is no source of regret, as I've heard some say, but rather of anticipation, that so much great reading awaits me. I've still not read *War and Peace*, nor Macaulay's *History of England*, nor Plutarch's *Lives*; I will some day. I have, though, recently read *Narrative of the Life of Frederick Douglass, an American Slave*, and just last week—for the first time, at age fifty-one—*Jane Eyre*, which I enjoyed greatly.

The eighty books I've written about for *Vintage Reading* include, by my count, thirty-eight American authors, five German or Austrian, five French, two Italian, and twenty-two British. Thirty-three are fiction, the rest nonfiction. Forty-seven first appeared after 1900, fifteen in the nineteenth century, eight in the previous three centuries, one in the early Christian era, nine in antiquity. Ten were penned by women, at least half a dozen by homosexuals, none by Hispanic authors, two by African-Americans. Eight have an Asian setting or "Eastern" flavor, four raise identifiably Jewish themes or subjects. One takes place on Mars. Books by tyrants, knaves, curmudgeons, and misanthropes number at least five. In a spirit of usefulness, I dutifully transmit the results of these calculations. I leave to others to figure out what they mean. ❖

# ONE

## *On Everyone's List of Literary Classics*

| | |
|---|---|
| *Look Homeward, Angel* | Thomas Wolfe |
| *The Portrait of a Lady* | Henry James |
| *As I Lay Dying* | William Faulkner |
| *Wuthering Heights* | Emily Bronte |
| *Kim* | Rudyard Kipling |
| *Alice's Adventures in Wonderland* | Lewis Carroll |
| *Justine* | Lawrence Durrell |
| *Oliver Twist* | Charles Dickens |
| *Pride and Prejudice* | Jane Austen |
| *A Passage to India* | E. M. Forster |
| *My Ántonia* | Willa Cather |
| *Madame Bovary* | Gustave Flaubert |

A sadly unadventurous grouping?

The truth is, the dozen novels here would land on almost anyone's list of admired classics. Oliver, Madame Bovary, White Rabbit, Kim, and the other characters who appear in them are by now almost no longer fictional; they live in our collective imagination. We encounter them, third hand, in the movies and plays most of these novels have inspired. But how much better to meet them personally, within the warm embrace of print, in the way Dickens and Flaubert intended us to meet them?

# Look Homeward, Angel

*By Thomas Wolfe*
*First published in 1929*

This is a Great American Novel.

Nothing about it is small. From its sheer length to its soaring, sometimes overswollen language, to its magnificent characters, to a romantic publishing history awash in the glow of a famous editor (Maxwell Perkins), to the towering narcissistic personality of its author, *Look Homeward Angel* is, and always was, a Literary Event.

Plot? The plot is that Eugene Gant is born and grows up, period. This is a coming-of-age novel, one relating Eugene's rich inner experience while growing up in a small southern city—"Altamont"—in the early years of the century. "A Story of the Buried Life," Wolfe subtitled it.

Eugene, set apart early from his brothers and sisters as the family scholar, inwardly thrills to the glories of the *Iliad* and of Shakespeare, dreams of maidens and warriors, virtue and purity. He feels confined and out of place in Altamont—"Oh, lost!" is Wolfe's refrain—but he is rescued from a life of unremembered dailiness by Mrs. Leonard, a kindly teacher and intellectual mentor.

Eugene's mother, Eliza Gant: No paragon of sweetness, she. Her mind forever clicking to a calculus of real estate deals, she sees Altamont as a gridwork of future roads and rising land prices. Her boardinghouse takes in everyone from part-time prostitutes to dying consumptives.

Eugene's father, Oliver Gant: A great human hulk of a man whom American literature will not soon forget, if only for his rolling diatribes, sometimes drunken and sometimes not, that thunder down and across the pages, lamenting his life, cursing his fate or his foes. As, for example, in this performance, delivered to hapless draymen who have dared to sprawl on the steps in front of his shop:

"You are the lowest of the low, the vilest of the vile. You lousy, good-for-nothing bums: You have brought me to the verge of starvation, you have frightened away the little business that might have put bread in my mouth, and kept the wolf from my door. By God, I hate you, for you stink a mile off. You low degenerates, you accursed reprobates; you would steal the pennies from a dead man's eyes, as you have from mine, fearful, awful, and bloodthirsty mountain grills that you are!"

And the setting for this Great American Novel, this would-be well-spring of the American character? Why Asheville, N.C., of all places, here named Altamont. If normally it's dangerous to term a novel autobiographical and proceed to search out exact correspondences between the author's fiction and his life, here they are indisputable. Thomas Wolfe's father was a stonecutter, his mother the proprietress of a boarding house; so is Eugene Gant's. Wolfe was precocious, well-read beyond his years, by all accounts a prodigy. So is Eugene Gant. Wolfe attended the University of North Carolina at Chapel Hill, Eugene the state university at Pulpit Hill.

Altamont is so unambiguously Asheville that following the book's appearance, Wolfe was sued for what amounted to malicious gossip. One woman wrote him that though she disapproved of lynching in general, she would not lift a hand were he dragged across the public square and strung from the nearest limb. For it was not the Asheville of its boosters that Wolfe described, but of pinch-mouthed landladies, and raging drunken brawls, and cross-racial "Niggertown" liaisons.

Today, half a century later, readers can experience Wolfe's Asheville in great outpourings of sentiment and grandiloquence, in riotous paragraphs that careen down the pages: Eugene "heard the ghostly ticking of his life; his powerful clairvoyance, the wild Scotch gift of Eliza, burned inward across the phantom years, plucking out the ghostly shadows of a million gleams of light—a little station by the rails at dawn, the road cleft through the pineland seen at twilight, a smoky cabin-light below the trestles, a boy who ran among the bounding calves, a wisp-haired slattern, with snuff-sticked mouth, framed in a door..."

Often it goes on for paragraph after paragraph like this, seemingly out of control, as if the author were determined to purge his soul, through language, of every thought, feeling or experience that ever was his. Any freshman composition teacher would edit it ruthlessly.

Still, Wolfe's great, rambling paragraphs stand in rough proportion to the job he sets them to do. His whole "project"—and if great dams, bridges and pipelines come to mind, that is not inappropriate—is animated by an ambitiousness of scale, a sense of its own importance, that wins us over by its sheer audacity. The writer takes his work dead seriously—the more so, no doubt, because his subject is so unabashedly himself.

Narcissistic? Sure. But then, Wolfe himself was large; he was six-foot-six. So is his story. ❖

# The Portrait of a Lady

*By Henry James*
*First published in 1881*

Everybody in this long, leisurely novel about expatriate American life in late nineteenth-century Europe loves Isabel Archer.

For starters, there's Caspar Goodwood, a Boston cotton mill owner with "a face like a grey February sky"—fixed, humorless, literal. There's Lord Warburton, prototype of English landed gentry, wealthy beyond measure, gracious and good, but muddled when it comes to women. There's Isabel's sickly cousin Ralph, master of irony, but the most brotherly to Isabel of any of them. And finally, the icily intelligent Gilbert Osmond, an aesthete who, never before moved to do anything in particular with his life, troubles himself to woo Isabel only at the urging of a former lover—the poised, serene, but endlessly calculating Madame Merle.

What a cast! And each of them sophisticated and many-layered, with not a straightforward bone in their bodies. Even silly, scatterbrained Countess Gemini, Osmond's sister, proves more complex than she seems, in the end serving up dark revelations to poor innocent Isabel.

They all love Isabel Archer, and no wonder; there's much to love. She's charming, unspoiled yet spirited, with a head full of fine ideas and great expectations. Lifted up from provincial Albany, New York, by her dry, acid-tongued Aunt Lydia, she's deposited at the English country home of her aunt's husband. There, in the glow of an English garden, Isabel first meets Europe, and the men and women who will fill her life for the story's next six years.

Isabel wishes to taste life without marriage getting in the way. She fears isolating herself, she declares, "from the usual chances and dangers, from what most people know and suffer." At one point, she rejects in the space of a week two marriage proposals, at least one of them a "brilliant" match by the standards of the day. "I don't need the aid of a clever man to teach me how to live," she tells one ardent suitor. What propels us through the novel's dense thicket of Jamesian prose is the wish to know how faithfully Isabel will cling to her convictions, whether any of her suitors will win her and what will become of her.

This is a novel you *can* put down; novels in 1881 had no television with which to compete, and this one's sentences wander as if you had all day to wander with them. In taking stock of her ruined marriage after its first fond beginnings, for example, Isabel finds that what she'd hoped would be "the infinite vista of a multiplied life" has turned into a dark alley; "Instead of leading to the high places of happiness, from which the world would seem to be below one, so that one could look down with a sense of exaltation and advantage, and judge and choose and pity, [her marriage] led rather downward and earthward, into realms of restriction and depression, where the sound of other lives, easier and freer, was heard as from above, and served to deepen the feeling of failure." Vintage James, all seventy-one words of it. His paragraphs sometimes leave a whole two-page spread black with type.

But if *Portrait's* paragraphs are long, its insights into motivation and character are correspondingly deep. This is, indeed, a "portrait" which darkens and deepens as Isabel, the innocent American caught up in the malevolent spell of Europe, discards the blinders of naivete. "Don't try to be good," Countess Gemini advises her. "Be a little wicked, feel a little wicked, for once in your life." Beneath the outward charm of these upper crust lives sizzles a cauldron of mistrust, jealousy and revenge, intricate plots, hidden pasts, and plain cruelty.

All *The Portrait of a Lady* lacks is sex. In a novel which otherwise so richly evokes personality, its absence is striking. How, one wonders, does the intimate life of Isabel and her husband reveal, if at all, early signs of the descending coldness? We see occasional hints of something other than conversational repartee between Osmond and his old lover, say; or Isabel's rough-hewn newspaper friend and her traveling companion. But there's only a single impetuous and passionate kiss in the whole book, and this after some five hundred pages. To a modern reader, it seems unnatural and archaic, a sad casualty of its times.

All the rest of this dense psychological portrait, however, seems as fresh and alive as dinner with one's most enchanting friend. ❖

# As I Lay Dying

*By William Faulkner*
*First published in 1930*

How to articulate the strangled voices of the inarticulate?
William Faulkner does it in *As I Lay Dying*.

In it, he writes of the death of Addie Bundren and her family's tragedy-burdened trek across back country Mississippi to bury her. The Bundrens bear washed out bridges, the drowning of their mules, fire, the duplicity of townspeople, and their own ignorance, while all the while Addie's corpse smolders under the southern sun and buzzards hover overhead.

Good story—yet it accounts for barely a hundredth's part of the novel's power. Much more resides in the intensely wrought inner lives of the family members—poor, unsophisticated, country folk not given to expressing much in the way of finer feelings, yet each of whom is granted life through Faulkner's artistry.

Anse, the father: Proud, stubbornly intent on hewing to his wife's dying wishes—and also on getting a new set of teeth, to "get my mouth fixed where I could eat God's own victuals as a man should."

Cash, one of four sons, patient coffin maker, hewer of beveled edges, philosopher of wood and life: "The animal magnetism of a dead body," he pronounces, in one of a numbered list of principles, "makes the stress come slanting, so the seams and joints of a coffin are made on the bevel."

Dewey Dell, the only daughter, seventeen and pregnant: "I feel like a wet seed wild in the hot blind earth."

Darl, the oldest son, whose eyes see more than the others, whose tangled brain ultimately hatches an act of mad impetuosity, and who is the instrument for much of Faulkner's literary virtuosity: As the brothers carry the coffin, "Cash begins to fall behind, hobbling to keep up, breathing harshly; then he is distanced and Jewel carries the entire front end alone, so that, tilting as the path begins to slant, it begins to rush away from me and slip down the air like a sled upon invisible snow, smoothly evacuating atmosphere..."

On one hand, Faulkner's story confirms stereotypes—of ignorant rural folk, barely touched by civilization, victims of their own dumb pride, getting into one impossible, sometimes funny scrape after another—the Keystone Kops of Yoknapatawpha County, Mississippi.

And yet Faulkner undermines stereotypes, too, laying to rest the conceit that maybe such people are not quite so human as the rest of us, are less "interesting," less deserving of our attention. Their minds may not work like those of more educated people. But their sensibilities are no less rich. And, in some ways, may be more so, their lives being so much closer to the growings and strainings and dyings of nature. Dewey Dell, alone in the night: "I feel the darkness rushing past my breast, past the cow; I begin to rush upon the darkness but the cow stops me and the darkness rushes on upon the sweet blast of her moaning breath, filled with wood and with silence."

*As I Lay Dying* is a simple story, of a simple family—told with elaborate fullness. Perspective shifts every few pages; each brief chapter has its own teller. Through the eyes of one character, the scene may be viewed as if through a cracked lens, distorted and obscured. Then, through another's, it comes into clearer view, the lens is reconstructed—granting a sense of discovery that is one of the novel's joys.

Faulkner is not easy reading. The scene shifts are one problem. Another is that he writes in what amounts to a foreign language, kin to standard English, but distant enough to sometimes make for heavy going: Anse tells how Vardaman, the youngest son, "comes around the house, bloody as a hog to his knees, and that ere fish chopped up with the axe like as not, or maybe throwed away for him to lie about the dog et it. Well,

I reckon I ain't no call to expect no more of him than of his mangrowed brothers."

Yes, the dialect demands work, at least for Yankee readers. But it's worth it, as a conduit to a world as exotic as that of Russian aristocracy, or Chinese peasantry, and no less compelling. ❖

# Wuthering Heights

*By Emily Brontë*
*First published in 1847*

In this dark story of passion and revenge in rural nineteenth-century England, not a single character gains our unmixed admiration.

Nelly, the housekeeper who narrates most of the story, is devious and expedient. Edgar, who ought to be the hero but isn't, is insipid and milk-blooded, his sister spoiled and silly. And these are the more agreeable residents of the drama. Compared to drunken Hindley or Bible-spouting old Joseph, they're almost appealing. And compared to Heathcliff, they're downright lovable.

Heathcliff towers over the Yorkshire moors like an avenging angel, a furious black cloud launching angry thunderbolts. "I have no pity!" he declares. "The more the worms writhe, the more I yearn to crush out their entrails! It's a moral teething; and I grind with greater energy, in proportion to the increase of pain."

This is no ordinary villain, but one of singular passion and ferocity, a villain's villain. Yet Emily Brontë's considerable art lets us sympathize with him. Picked up off the Liverpool streets, Heathcliff—just "Heathcliff"; he has no other name—is raised on the family estate, Wuthering Heights. He is treated well while Earnshaw, the master of the house, yet lives. But upon his death, the boy comes under the cruel dominion of Earnshaw's son, Hindley, who humiliates him.

Hindley's sister Catherine, though, shows him kindness. The two become fast friends. The friendship ripens into love. But Catherine's more conventional match to Edgar Linton, who lives across the moor at Thrushcross Grange—that's the name, really!—frustrates Heathcliff's love and completes the hardening of his heart. The rest of the story relates

Heathcliff's deepening, mad passion for his childhood friend and his revenge on those he feels have wronged him.

"Wuthering," we learn, is "a significant provincial adjective, descriptive of the atmospheric tumult to which its station is exposed in stormy weather...One may guess the power of the north wind blowing over the edge by the excessive slant of a few stunted firs at the end of the house; and by a range of gaunt thorns all stretching their limbs one way, as if craving alms of the sun." In this stark country, by turns indescribably lovely and savage, the action of the novel takes place. (From it, too, Emily Brontë herself never ventured far for long.)

It is lonely country, largely unpeopled, unsoftened by the civilizing influence of great towns, and the reader sometimes cringes at its emotional claustrophobia. From Wuthering Heights to Thrushcross Grange and back again, sometimes to the moor between, the action alternates, always under Heathcliff's malevolent spell. One gasps for fresher, happier air. The characters inhabit an unpolluted rural paradise; yet they're as chained by human passion and weakness as men and women anywhere.

Maybe more so. As the town-bred visitor, Lockwood, observes: "The people in these regions...live more in earnest, more in themselves, and less in surface change, and frivolous external things." There is less to dissipate consuming emotion and in such a setting the hate in dark Heathcliff can fester: "It's odd what a savage feeling I have to anything that seems afraid of me! Had I been born where laws are less strict, and tastes less dainty, I should treat myself to a slow vivisection of those two, as an evening's entertainment." "Those two," be it noted, are his own son and his son's future bride.

Deeply theatrical all this is, and Brontë's musical prose is often borne along on cadences that verge on the Shakespearean. "Come to the glass and I'll let you see what you should wish," young Heathcliff is instructed. "Do you mark these two lines between your eyes? And those thick brows, that instead of rising arched, sink in the middle?...Wish and learn to smooth away the surly wrinkles."

No, these characters hardly speak as we imagine people—even English gentry of a century and a half ago—would speak. And such high-flown language coupled with, perhaps, overdrawn characters, offers the parodist a rich vein of material.

So, why read it today? When first published (under the authorship of one "Currer Bell") in 1847, few did. It and *Jane Eyre*, by Emily's sister Charlotte, both appeared in the same year. But it was to the latter that the English reading public flocked. "To enter fully into the spirit" of *Wuthering Heights*, one critic has noted, "the reader needs to face a truth more disquieting than the surface verisimilitude of *Jane Eyre*. The Victorian public was not ready to face this truth."

Are we? That goodness not allowed to grow can mutate into evil, and that behind great cruelty may once have dwelt great love, is the brutal, essential lesson of *Wuthering Heights*. ❖

# *Kim*

### By Rudyard Kipling
### First published in 1901

Kim's father, a hard-drinking, opium-smoking member of His Majesty's Army in India, dies when he is still a child. His mother long dead of cholera, he grows up with British blood and an Indian soul in the streets of Lahore. As the story opens, he meets an ancient lama (a Buddhist monk) while sitting outside the city's antiquities museum.

The lama has embarked on a quest for the river sprung from Buddha's arrow: "Whoso bathes in it washes away all taint and speckle of sin." The boy, too, is on a personal quest—for what he grows up hearing called a red bull on a green field, the insignia of his father's Irish regiment. The two take up with one another and set out upon the Grand Trunk Road that stretches across India. Kim becomes the lama's *chela*, or disciple—washes his feet, begs for him.

But Rudyard Kipling's *Kim* is no tale of spiritual questing. As attached as he is to the lama, Kim remains a sharp-eyed denizen of back alley and bazaar. Indeed, so abruptly does the novel deposit us in the distant and exotic East, that we're taken aback when we realize that it actually qualifies as that familiar literary genre, the spy-adventure story. For Kim, we learn, is in the service of Mahbub Ali, horse trader and spy; he is to play a central role in a major undercover operation, in a war with five native kings, and in international intrigue involving the Russians and the French.

As for the lama, for all his talk about the Wheel of Life and the River of the Arrow, you never really know whether he's a genuinely spiritual figure, a sly old codger or slightly daft.

Suffusing the story, of course, is India in the days of the Raj, of crowded bazaars and grimly third-class railway coaches. We come upon isolated huts in the foothills of the Himalayas; upon a marriage procession, with "music and shoutings, and a smell of marigold and jasmine stronger even than the reek of the dust."

*Kim* must have seemed exotic indeed to British readers of the turn of the century. For American readers, twice removed by time, place and sensibilities, it's twice exotic—and sometimes twice hard. You often have the uneasy sense that you're getting by, but only barely, in a foreign language, missing every fourth word.

Kipling was born in Bombay of British parents and lived much of his early life in India; to him *England* was exotic. He wrote, at age thirty-seven: "I am slowly discovering England, which is the most wonderful foreign land I have ever been in." So in *Kim*, he imparts the experience of inhabiting what to him was home, but which to us is foreign. We confront names and places, like Ferozepore, Umballa, and Mian Mir; a plethora of words, like *chela, sepoy,* and *naik.*

Most alien of all are speech patterns foreign to our ears, where Kipling represents the vernacular through odd constructions and archaic language. Thus, one conversation comes out like this:

"Two men wait thy coming behind the horse-trucks," Kim warns Mahbub. "They will shoot thee at thy lying down, because there is a price on thy head. I heard, sleeping near the horses."

"Didst thou see them?...Hold still, Sire of Devils?" This furiously to the horse.

"No."

"Was one dressed belike as a faquir?"

"One said to the other, 'What manner of faquir art thou, to shiver at a little watching?"

The effect is plainly intentional, for speech among British officers, for example, gives us a sudden rush of ease and familiarity, as in overhearing wisps of American English in a foreign airport.

Like much of Tom Wolfe's work in our day, *Kim* is a novel of surfaces, full of dress, talk, action. We are insiders, as it were, to the busy
public life of the Grand Trunk Road—yet outsiders to the internal lives
of the characters. Even interior monologues leave us inhabiting the outskirts of mind and heart, not the center of the soul. Mahbub Ali remains
a mystery. The lama is a mystery. Kim is a mystery.

India is a mystery.

*Kim* does not satisfy our appetite for the East so much as whet it. ❖

ROBERT KANIGEL

# Alice's Adventures in Wonderland

*By Lewis Carroll*
*First published in 1865*

Prim little girl meets hyperactive White Rabbit and chases him down a rabbit hole. She drinks various potions, grows larger and smaller. Meets inquisitorial caterpillar, baby-nursing duchess, grinning Cheshire cat. Attends tea party with assortment of insane guests. Plays croquet with King and Queen, using live flamingo as croquet mallet...

These are some of *Alice's Adventures in Wonderland,* and all that's wrong with Lewis Carroll's inspired dream story is that it ends too soon. Even this fault, though, has a remedy: Seven years after its first appearance came a sequel, *Through the Looking Glass,* that some feel actually improved on the original.

The Alice stories have been psychoanalyzed, plumbed for hidden political and religious messages, even probed for roots in their creator's affinity for mathematics and logic. But no tired theorizing can explain their enduring appeal to generations of children and adults. They are endlessly inventive. Their characters are unforgettable. They are, simply, great fun. As one critic has pointed out, Lewis Carroll "did not send Alice down the rabbit hole on a summer's afternoon for the benefit of a future generation of Freudians, but rather for the present pleasure of three Victorian children."

Charles Lutwidge Dodgson was a mathematician, author of a number of scholarly treatises. He was a deacon in the Church of England. He was an ardent and accomplished photographer—in one critic's view, "the best photographer of children in the nineteenth century." Yet today we remember him for none of this. For in 1862, he and an adult friend went on a boat trip upriver from Oxford with three children—ten-year-old

Alice Liddell being one of them—during which he told the story that turned into *Alice's Adventures in Wonderland*. Three years later, it was published under a pseudonym, Lewis Carroll.

Happily, the published version retained much of the spontaneity and madcap inventiveness of the original. It is supremely clever, in the best sense of the word. It's full of delightful puns, poems scattered amidst the prose, and typographical high jinks—as when the text of the Mouse's tale winds down the page in the form of a tail. And it boasts a cast of outrageous characters, every one of whom is fully developed: It's not *any* rabbit Alice meets, but a nervous and silly one, dressed in kid gloves and waistcoat. It's not *any* cook that Alice encounters at the Duchess's, but one with a penchant for throwing frying pans.

This would-be children's story is not all sweetness and light: A strain of danger and uncertainty winds through it, as if to subtly raise the emotional stakes. The Queen of Hearts, for example, is a kind of Stalin of children's literature, forever ordering "Off with his head" at any imagined affront. The blue caterpillar Alice meets lolling atop the mushroom is sarcastic and forbidding. Even the neurotic White Rabbit is nobody you'd want to spend much time with.

But then there's Alice herself, an island of calm amid all the madness, ever rational, slow to anger, a model of Victorian girlhood. "Curiouser and curiouser," Alice may be heard to say. Or, "How queer everything is today." But for her, Wonderland is no fearful hocus-pocus world of superstition and terror, but merely the place, just a tad out of kilter, in which she happens to find herself.

The mushroom on which Alice nibbles to fine-tune her size is not "magic," merely a mushroom. She approaches everything with curiosity and uncommon common sense. Any child, I suspect, would come away from reading her adventures more apt and better able to find wonder in the world than shrink in terror from its dangers.

So would any adult not irreversibly ground down by "maturity's" stern demands. ❖

# *Justine*

*By Lawrence Durrell*
*First published in 1957*

When it first appeared in the nineteen-fifties, *Justine* could be judged wholly on its face—as a lush, sensuous novel of love steeped in the sights and scents of a corrupt and teeming Egyptian city. Today, it is known, too, as the first panel in that textured literary tapestry known as *The Alexandria Quartet*.

Readers of *Justine* today, then, are apt to have lost some literary innocence. They likely know that the same cast of remarkable characters will reappear in the subsequent volumes, *Balthazar, Mountolive* and *Clea*, their motivations reinterpreted, their personalities grown richer and more rounded; that many of them lead double and triple lives; that there's more to Justine's infidelity to her princely Egyptian husband than is ever revealed here. As one writer has put it, *The Alexandria Quartet* is a "serial drama that, instead of steadily advancing, continuously folds in on itself." Only in *Clea*, the final book, does the action move ahead in time.

The tetralogy takes its title from the sense-dripping, often suffocating city in which it is set and which—a bit self-consciously to my taste—functions as a central character. In fact, the real terrain for the *Quartet* is love, its endless variations, its subtleties of feeling, its refusal to resolve itself into anything simpler than what it is. Alexandria is the test tube for love, brimming over with all the ingredients needed for its study.

*Justine*: A writer named Darley, already involved with Melissa, takes up with the haunted Justine, wife of Nessim, a wealthy merchant. Their affair progresses against a backdrop of intrigue and one-of-a-kind characters: the Cabalist Balthazar; "the gentle, lovable, unknowable Clea"; and the one-eyed Scobie, a wrinkled old police functionary.

Near the end, Nessim holds a duck shoot; a man is killed. Then Justine, the object of at least two men's ardor, goes to Palestine, settling on a kibbutz. "Watching her now and remembering the touching and tormenting person she had once been for us all," Clea writes Darley, "I found it hard to comprehend the change into this tubby little peasant with the hard paws..."

But only gradually does this seeming wisp of a story develop. Durrell has called himself "a poet who stumbled into prose," and the description is apt: Lyrical evocations of Alexandria and its bizarre denizens find favored treatment in Durrell's hands, while the story line suffers by comparison. Dialogue is stylized, not to say stilted, and never overly concerned with moving the narrative ahead. Readers inured to a story that hurtles along may be disappointed.

The places and events Darley records are of his past, forced through the prism of memory. They come out in ill-ordered, self-contained snatches—soft, glowing, emotionally heightened, as if through a cinematographer's hazy filter: "The whole room belonged to Melissa—the pitiful dressing-table full of empty powder-boxes and photos: the graceful curtain breathing softly in that breathless afternoon air like the sail of a ship. How often had we not lain in one another's arms watching the slow intake and recoil of that transparent piece of bright linen? Across all this, as across the image of someone dearly loved, held in the magnification of a gigantic tear, moved the brown harsh body of Justine naked."

Sometimes, all this good stuff is too much—too many colors, textures, smells—and interest flags. More often, it is gently hypnotic, like a drug. In fact the whole book can be likened to certain hypnotics that heighten sensory sensitivity but then, in time, give way to a sweet narcosis, like that of a lazy noonday nap in summer grass under a warming sun. ❖

# Oliver Twist

*By Charles Dickens*
*First published in 1838*

It is overwritten, moralistic and hopelessly sentimental, with turns of plot that would make a writer of romance novels blush. But cavil all you like about the literary shortcomings of *Oliver Twist*, it is inspired by a warmth and appreciation for sheer human goodness not often seen today.

An infant delivered even as its mother dies, in the rudest and most miserable surroundings, gets the name Oliver Twist—by virtue of the letter T following the S of a child named Swubble. He grows up in the workhouse, unloved and half-starved, is apprenticed to an undertaker, finally runs off to London. There, he falls in with a gang of pickpockets and thieves led by the inimitable Fagin. On a venture with his new friends, of whose criminal activities he is unaware, he's arrested for a pickpocketing committed by another. Miraculously, he is found innocent; a witness comes forward to substantiate his story, and the victim of the crime sees in young Oliver a sweetness and nobility of character inconsistent with a criminal heart.

All through the story, similar forces work on Oliver, good and evil competing for his fate. Despite his grimy dress and criminal surroundings, his innocence endears him to respectable folk—a trait Fagin sees as making him ideal for a life of crime; who, after all, would suspect so sweet a boy?

Oddly, Oliver sometimes seems a minor character in the novel that bears his name. His early years in the workhouse are drawn sympathetically enough. But later, flung back and forth between Fagin and the kindhearted men and women who would rescue him, he's more object than subject. We know that all are taken with his innocence, that he acknowledges the kindness of his benefactors, that he resists Fagin's path of cruelty and crime. But we never know how he feels deep down as fortune subjects him to its whims.

*Oliver Twist* is a social document, and a troubling one. Keenly aware of social ills, it launches frequent barbs at the treatment of the poor. Yet, a deep conservative streak runs through it, too. Criminals, bumblers and hypocrites seem drawn exclusively from the lower social classes, while Oliver's benefactors are invariably the soul of upper middle class respectability, people who would today drive Volvos. How much, one wonders, does this split owe to social conditions, how much to innate character? Are Fagin, robber Bill Sikes and the rest of the gang victims of the System—or just plain bad?

The question torments us today as much as in Dickens' time. For just as then, we have a great underclass, from which few seem able to extricate themselves, whose poverty, criminal behavior and despair mock middle class values. Is it their own fault, we wonder, or ours? Does the continued existence of an underclass suggest that, reformers to the contrary, nothing much can be done about it? Or that our society stands indicted of just not caring?

Dickens' novel is ambivalent in its answers. On the one hand, Oliver's strength of character is made to seem the product of the superior stock from which, we learn, he derives; blood, in other words, tells. But what of Nancy, Bill Sikes' moll? At one point, given a chance to step out from her dissolute life and into a new, more hopeful one, she refuses. Why? Because of the awful hold of the underworld upon her? Or because of her own weakness of character?

*Oliver Twist* raises other troubling questions, not the least of which is anti-Semitism. Fagin, the sly, malevolent and miserly leader of the gang, who is happy to see his own henchmen swing from the gallows if it will save his skin, is a Jew; by itself, nothing anti-Semitic in that. But a modern reader's tolerance wears thin when Fagin is repeatedly referred to not by name but simply as "the Jew." Fagin never suffers a single taunt about his Jewishness from either the assorted low-lifes who populate the novel, or anyone else. Nor does Dickens ever attribute his vicious nature to it. And yet if Fagin is just an evil man who happens to be Jewish, why that ugly, incessant chorus—*the Jew*?

In reading *Oliver Twist*, one does not reach for the word "great"; the novel is too resolutely middle class to inspire the word. For all its preoccupation with sordid city streets, it glories in the joys of hearth and home. And—as in a minor character's decision to renounce ambition and opt for a parsonage in the country—it seems to reject anything too high flown, as well.

Fagin's defeat, and Oliver's salvation, represent a victory for ordinary lives lived quietly and well. ❖

# Pride and Prejudice

*By Jane Austen*
*First published in 1813*

Though afflicted by a title reminiscent of a Horatio Alger story or a Sunday school tract, *Pride and Prejudice* is a love story. And largely because it leaves you in the extended company of one of the most appealing and intelligent characters in all of fiction, Elizabeth Bennet, it's a delight to read.

A young and spirited upper-class woman in early nineteenth-century England, Elizabeth meets the sullen and mysterious Mr. Fitzwilliam Darcy. She immediately dislikes him for his apparent conceit and disdain for social niceties. But gradually, over the span of the book, her feelings change. This slow reversal is fascinating in itself, if only for the psychologically precise insights it affords into how people come to hold the impressions they do, and how they may come to give them up. Indeed, substance and appearance are as much the twin subject of Jane Austen's novel as pride and prejudice.

This is a novel of manners. Nothing much happens. No bloody revolutions upset the world its characters inhabit, no civil strife, no hunger, no physical danger. The characters amiably converse. Or stroll through well-tended gardens. Or attend balls. Politics never intrudes. Neither does the need to make a living. The characters worry only about living up to the mandates of their class—to marry well, live comfortably, and speak in a civil tone of voice.

At first blush, all this might seem wholly irrelevant to all the rest of us who daily strive and struggle. And yet, the serene, ordered backdrop of these characters' lives means that whatever takes place against it stands out in bold relief. Lines of action are clear, clean and spare, without workaday reality to muddy up matters. Personality traits are high-lighted. Emotional intensity gets a chance to irresistibly build; for sheer sexual tension, few novels can match that moment when Elizabeth suddenly encounters Darcy at his family home: "Their eyes instantly met, and the cheeks of each were overspread with the deepest blush."

The story is unusually rich in memorable supporting characters. Like the clergyman Collins, whose bouts of long-winded flattery offer intervals of comic relief (especially when he proposes to Elizabeth). And the high-born Lady Catherine de Bourgh, whose brusque imperiousness could forment a revolution. And Elizabeth's older sister Jane, who can say no unkind word of anyone. Or their mother, Mrs. Bennet, a nervous, silly woman whose only wish is to see her five daughters married off—at whatever cost to her own dignity, such as it is.

Modern readers may at first resist this world of exaggerated manners and verbal artifice. But for most, it won't be long before all that recedes into the background and the story itself takes hold. That story's superficial aspect is pleasant, light and airy. But by contrast, it renders the darker, deeper relationship between such substantial characters as Fitzwilliam Darcy and Elizabeth Bennet serious indeed, compelling our interest almost two centuries after Jane Austen brought them to life. ❖

# A Passage to India

*By E. M. Forster*
*First published in 1924*

*A Passage to India* fictionally portrays the clash of cultures between Indians and their British masters during the twilight years of the Empire. It takes the abstraction that is "colonialism" and reveals it for the darkly brutal force it's often been.

In a mysterious, fevered moment deep in the caves of Marabar, young Adela Quested, fresh from England, fancies that her Indian acquaintance, Assiz, has tried to rape her. While just what did happen in the cave is never made clear—an ambiguity that Forster plainly means to stand for the mysteries of the East—it is clear that Assiz is innocent. The English authorities rally 'round the aggrieved victim of oriental depravity and, with evident relish, bring the case to trial. But then, on the witness stand, in a moment of crystalline insight, Adela recants her story.

The victim of her confusion, Assiz, is a medical doctor, intelligent and capable. But he is also exquisitely temperamental, his Western scientific training but a thin veneer laid down upon a mystical and poetic streak that holds kindness above justice, reason, consistency or truth.

For Assiz, Forster writes, there was "no harm in deceiving society as long as she does not find you out, because it is only when she finds you out that you have harmed her; she is not like a friend or God, who are injured by the mere existence of unfaithfulness. [And so], he meditated what type of lie he should tell..."

At least in Forster's telling, the petty falsehoods of Assiz and the Indians generally are like the lies told the dying cancer patient; they insulate against painful truth, protect fragile feelings. To Indians, "unless a sentence paid a few compliments to Justice and Morality in passing, its grammar wounded their ears and paralysed their minds. What they said and what they felt were (except in the case of affection) seldom the same."

To the English, who understand none of this, it is all quite simple: The "natives" are duplicitous, unworthy of social contact beyond the merest pleasantries. If the density of prejudice heaped on them here is based even roughly on historical fact, it's a wonder the Indians didn't throw off their shackles long before they did. If anything, English women act most callously of all. "Why, the kindest thing one can do to a native is to let them die," says Mrs. Callendar, wife of the chief medical officer. She's content so long as the Indians "don't come near me. They give me the creeps."

Almost alone among the English to see the Indians as different rather than inferior is Cyril Fielding, principal of the government college. He and Assiz become friends, though the cultural chasm yawns wide; their relationship is ambivalent, strained, easy prey to misunderstanding. Assiz's problem with Fielding is that, though more comfortable among Indians than with his English compatriots, Fielding is still an Englishman. Only in tender moments can Assiz forgive him that. "He knew at the bottom of his heart that [the English] could not help being so cold and odd and circulating like an ice stream through his land."

Offering another variation-on-an-Englishman theme is city magistrate Ronn Heaslop, the man whose merits as marriage partner Adela has come to India to weigh. He's as scornful of the natives as the others, but less blindly. "I am out here to work," he says, "to hold this wretched country by force. I'm not a missionary or a Labour Member or a vague sentimental sympathetic literary man. I'm just a servant of the Government."

A Passage to India works as both a great tapestry of India and through its small, sharp insights. And it is prophetic, too. In the end, rejecting European ways and European medicine, Assiz retreats from British India. "I am an Indian at last," he tells himself. "Clear out," he tells Fielding in what each knows will be their last meeting. "Why are we [Indians] put to so much suffering? We used to blame you, now we blame ourselves, we grow wiser. Until England is in difficulties, we keep silent, but in the next European war—aha, aha! Then is our time."

The next European war was World War II, which ended in 1945. By 1948, Gandhi and Nehru had wrested India from the Crown. ❖

ROBERT KANIGEL

# *My Ántonia*

*By Willa Cather*
*First published in 1918*

This long-time staple of high school required reading lists includes, by my count, one out-of-wedlock pregnancy, two suicides, and three murders. Yet these are the last elements of Willa Cather's *My Ántonia* one would ever remember or remark on. Somehow, they evoke in the reader no revulsion, seem little more than dark ornamentation to a sunny story of growing up on the American plains in the waning years of the nineteenth century.

A Virginia boy whose parents have both recently died, Jim Burden goes to live with his grandparents on the Nebraska prairie. There he's thrown into a culture of recent immigrants from Scandinavia and central Europe. There he meets Ántonia Shimerda, a girl from Bohemia, a region of what we now call the Czech Republic.

"Tony," as he calls her, lives in a mud house on a nearby farm. She works in the fields while still young, as a "hired girl" in town when a little older. She runs off with a no 'count railway conductor who gets her pregnant and then deserts her. Later she marries a solid, gentle man named Anton Cuzak and bears him a brood of kids.

*My Ántonia* is Jim's story of his boyhood friend. It is a book free of artifice, plainly written, ornamented only by the author's love for the land. "Style" has been stripped away, leaving the straightforward story itself. The plot's more sensational turns—those murders and suicides, for instance—usually take place off stage while the quiet, almost uneventful lives of Jim and "his" Ántonia occupy stage center.

The wholesome solidity of a book like this risks being lost on high school sophomores raised on Pepsi commercials and shopping mall glitter. So little happens to Ántonia; mainly, she works—and hard, unromantic, callus-thickening work it is at that. Might Cather's novel, one wonders, be pitched to teens as science fiction? For surely a world of mud houses, backyard chicken neck-wringing, and winter coats made from wolfskin must seem at least as foreign to today's young as men from Mars.

"Burning summers when the world lies green and billowy beneath a brilliant sky, when one is fairly stifled in vegetation, in the color and smell of strong weeds and heavy harvests; blustery winters with little snow, when the whole country is stripped bare and grey as sheet-iron." These are Cather's prairie lands. They are not—like the forbidding Yorkshire moors of *Wuthering Heights*, say—quite strong enough to function as a lead character. On the other hand, they are more than mere decoration. They are a backdrop against which character emerges and personality is starkly drawn.

Ántonia is direct, solid, unaffected, her English pleasingly overlaid with a central European inflection. For Jim Burden she represents all that's vigorous and pure about his prairie boyhood. Indeed, a case could be made that the novel is less about Ántonia—who says relatively little, figures in surprisingly little of the action and is, in fact, absent for lengthy stretches—than about the narrator and his love for her.

A haunting prologue launches the story. In it, a third party—an old friend of Jim's from Nebraska—tells how the book manuscript came to her attention. How she and Jim, by now "legal counsel for one of the great Western railways," had once, while crossing Iowa on the same train, reminisced about their Nebraska childhoods. How the conversation kept drifting back to the robust, dark-skinned Bohemian girl they both once knew. How Jim mentioned he'd been recording what he remembered about Ántonia, and that he would let her read it once he finished it.

"Months afterward," this third party—presumably a New York editor like Willa Cather herself—writes, "Jim called at my apartment one stormy winter afternoon, carrying a legal portfolio. He brought it into the sitting-room with him, and said, as he stood warming his hands, 'Here is the thing about Ántonia. Do you still want to read it?'"

She did.

We do. ❖

# Madame Bovary

*By Gustave Flaubert*
*First published in 1857*

Her heart thrilled to historical romances. She yearned to be swept away by a man of wealth and refinement, to feel her pulse race with reckless passion. She dreamed of being wed at midnight, by torchlight. She was the unforgettable Madame Bovary, and Gustave Flaubert's novel of that name became an immediate sensation when it was published in 1857.

But it was almost never published at all. Serializing it first in a popular magazine, the author was tried for "committing an outrage against public and religious morality." He won, and in gratitude dedicated the novel to his lawyer. But his story posed so conspicuous a threat to domestic peace that it's easy to see why the authorities were incensed.

Madame Bovary, you see, finds her marriage to Charles, a well-meaning drudge of a provincial doctor, insufficiently exciting. She succumbs to the blandishments of the dashing Rodolphe, who plots his sexual conquests with a chessmaster's finesse. Their tempestuous affair comes replete with fevered love letters left folded in the chinks of the garden wall. When the relationship ends, Madame Bovary takes up with Leon, a young law clerk. They meet in "their" room in a waterfront hotel in Rouen every Thursday while poor, stupid Charles thinks she's taking piano lessons; Madame Bovary gets the piano teacher to prepare fake bills. During none of these amorous escapades, needless to say, does Madame Bovary have much time for Berthe, her little girl.

Not a nice person, you say? Flaubert's achievement is to make you care about a character so seemingly weak, shallow, and mean of spirit.

But is Madame Bovary's conduct really so surprising? When one of her lovers laments being stuck out in the provinces, life passing him by, Madame Bovary points out that he's "scarcely to be pitied...After all, you're free." As a woman, she is not—and knows it. Indeed, one might argue that for a bourgeois woman then, an offer of marriage from a suitor with Charles' credentials was one she could hardly refuse. How could she know that, in wedding's wake, she would lament: Is this all there is?

A man, Madame Bovary feels, ought to "know everything, excel in all sorts of activities, initiate you into the turbulence of passion, the refinements and mysteries of life." Yet Charles' "conversation was as flat as a sidewalk," and his ideas, such as they were, appealed "to neither the emotions, the sense of humor, nor the imagination." What a contrast to the men she'd met in her fictional romances! Can we entirely blame her for finding pleasure in the arms of another man? Does it attest to a kind of strength that she is unwilling to settle for her lot? And does it not make *Madame Bovary* a profoundly conservative novel that she is so soundly punished for her behavior?

Maybe that's how Flaubert's lawyer got him off the hook—by pointing out that for her machinations, deceits and infidelities, Madame Bovary did indeed get her due.

Her fall begins once she agrees to a plan by Charles' creditor to secure power of attorney over his financial affairs. Charles blindly signs it, and it's downhill from then on. Behind his back, she spends more and more to satisfy her whims and feed her adultery; in the meantime, the House of Bovary sinks into the mire. Ultimately, notes fall due, the creditors won't extend them and the whole edifice topples, Madame Bovary with it.

Early on, the modern reader may have trouble slowing down enough to ease into the novel's provincial life. But gradually that world, initially a blur, slips into sharper focus. There, in Yonville, a stagecoach ride from Rouen, we meet Lomais, a pharmacist with intellectual pretensions who pens sly pieces for the local journal, hates the Church, fancies himself knowledgeable in every field, and deems it his duty to advise all the world of his opinions. Then there's the village priest, Bournisien, with whom Lomais continually wrangles (though in a long night of talk and drink they express affection for one another). And of course there's the dry goods merchant and part-time usurer, Lheureux, the instrument of Madame Bovary's undoing.

Mere types? Better, I think, to call them prototypes—the originals from which later copies derive. So convincingly are they drawn that, steeped in the life of the novel, you could return to Yonville, take a room at the inn and settle into the life of the village as if you had always lived there.

But do watch out for Madame Bovary. ❖

# TWO

## On Many a List for Burning

### Heretics, Outlaws, and Demagogues

| | |
|---|---|
| *Stories* | Dorothy Parker |
| *The Prince* | Niccolo Machiavelli |
| *The Devil's Dictionary* | Ambrose Bierce |
| *Mein Kampf* | Adolf Hitler |
| *Nana* | Emile Zola |
| *Ten Days That Shook the World* | John Reed |
| *Native Son* | Richard Wright |

---

Evil fascinates. Somehow, the subversive, heretical, vicious, and cruel grip the imagination.

This section encompasses everything from misanthropic short stories, to a curmudgeonly "dictionary" that reeks of bile, to a first-hand account of a revolution many saw as ushering in the Apocalypse, to venomous outpourings of raw hatred that even today cannot fail to shock.

# Stories

*By Dorothy Parker*
*First collected in book form, 1942*

If the stories she wrote during her lifetime shed light on her soul, Dorothy Parker was downright wicked.

In "Lady of the Lamp," one of two dozen stories appearing in one early collection of her work, a woman visits Mona, presumably her dear friend, in the hospital. Mona insists she's not sick, that it's just her nerves. "Just your nerves?" replies the friend, whose side of the conversation is the only one we hear. Plainly, she knows something she's not supposed to know.

"I'd thought it rather funny I hadn't heard from you, but you know how you are—you simply let people go, and weeks can go by like, well, *weeks*, and never a sign from you... Now, I'm not going to scold you when you're sick, but frankly..."

The emotional stakes escalate. "Oh, Mona dear, so often I think if you just had a home of your own...I worry so about you, living in a little furnished apartment, with nothing that belongs to you, no roots, no nothing. It's not right for a woman."

The sly barbs and wily insinuations begin to wreak their toll. "Why, Mona Morrison, are you crying? Oh, you've got a cold?...I thought you were crying there for a second."

What poor Mona needs to do, says her visitor, is marry. "It would be all the difference in the world. I think a child would do everything for you, Mona...Mona, baby, you really have got a rotten cold, haven't you? Don't you want me to get you another handkerchief?"

It becomes clear that Mona has had an abortion, that the visitor knows, that the visitor wishes to let her know she knows and that the visitor is out to destroy Mona's composure, dignity and self-esteem. "Mona, for heaven's sake! Don't scream like that. I'm not deaf, you know."

The taunts and stabs are so subtle, clothed in caring and concern, that their emotional violence is not at first apparent. And yet "Lady of the Lamp" is a full-blown horror story, with all that genre's sense of mounting terror. By the end, Mona is reduced to a shrinking, miserable rag of distraught emotion—whereupon her visitor, having achieved her end, calls in the doctor.

Dorothy Parker, a poet and critic as well as storyteller, presided over a court of literary wits that frequented Manhattan's Algonquin Hotel during the 1920s. Mona's visitor is like most of the characters appearing in her stories; there's scarcely a good, sweet, sensitive soul in the lot.

In "Horsie," a baby's nurse is cursed with large, indelicate features; her employers tease her mercilessly behind her back, all but waiting for her to whinny. In "Glory in the Daytime," Lily Wynton, a legendary actress, turns out to be a sad and sodden alcoholic, given to drunken recitations of her past roles. Then there's Hazel Morse, the "Big Blonde" of the story's title, who drifts from man to man, speakeasy to speakeasy, devoid of all sense of who she is, or of any talent but being company to men.

Why drop down into Parker's underworld of snide, shallow and otherwise unlikable characters? It's not fun, I'll tell you, though it is perversely fascinating. That's one reason to lap up her stories.

To harmlessly satisfy a sadistic streak? That's a second.

To study a consummate master in the cruel craft of dissecting human frailty might be a third. ❖

# The Prince

*By Niccolo Machiavelli*
*First published in 1537*

MACHIAVELLIAN, *adj.* Following the methods recommended by Machiavelli in preferring expediency to morality; duplicity in statecraft or general conduct.

That's what the word meant in 1592, when the *Oxford English Dictionary* records its appearance in the phrase "pestilent Machiavellian policie," and that's what it means today. Its impressive constancy of meaning owes much to this slim book, *The Prince*, and to the force and single-mindedness of its message.

Which is that politics and power are one thing, morality and ethics something else.

The Inquisition ordered Machiavelli's works destroyed. Mussolini chose *The Prince* as the subject of his doctoral thesis. Lenin and Stalin studied it, and Hitler reputedly kept it for bedtime reading. Is it, then, a work of evil, and thus not fit reading for all who ally themselves with good?

As a matter of fact, even Machiavelli allied himself with good. A Florentine statesman who lived from 1469 to 1532, Niccolo Machiavelli cared passionately about the fate of Italy and held important diplomatic posts with the Florentine Republic. He wrote *The Prince* while banished to a country villa when out of favor. In it, he never argued for evil over good, hatred over love, war over peace. He simply observed that any ruler inclined to retain his kingdom and achieve his political ends ought not give misguided obeisance to mere ethics.

*The Prince* is a practical textbook, a guide on how to rule. Chapter five, for example, tells "The Way to Govern Cities or Dominions That,

Previous to Being Occupied, Lived Under Their Own Laws." Chapter seventeen is entitled "Of Cruelty and Clemency and Whether It Is Better to Be Loved or Feared." Only the book's frequent references to the byzantine politics of early sixteenth-century Italy make its advice anything less than instantly relevant to the modern student of power.

Machiavelli points out that too-liberal policies may drain the public treasury and thus prompt unrest and widespread misery more readily than "niggardly" policies that preserve the state's financial health. Sound familiar? He writes that an assassination attempt, "which proceeds from the deliberate action of a determined man cannot be avoided." And he insists that, in the long run, the occasionally cruel prince "will be more merciful than those who, for excess of tenderness, allow disorders to arise, from whence spring bloodshed and rapine."

*The Prince* may be read today as a treatise on men and women in groups generally, and many of its prescriptions seem no less applicable to the corporate boardroom than to the halls of government: "There is no other way of guarding one's self against flattery than by letting men understand that they will not offend you by speaking the truth," is surely a constructive insight. A bit more questionable: "It is much safer to be feared than loved."

Machiavelli's air of supreme self-assurance surely owes much to the clean lines of his prose—whose virtues, as critic Kenneth Rexroth once noted, "survive all but the worst translations"—which comes across not as self-consciously "stylish" but elegant and pure. And pithy, as in: "It is the nature of men to be as much bound by the benefits that they confer as by those they receive."

Do not be too quick to condemn Signor Machiavelli. His divorce of politics from ethics inevitably leads to statements easily construed as callous or cynical—which, of course, they are. Yet the man himself plainly felt it was better to be good than evil, kind than cruel, on the side of God than of the Devil. And when it suited him, he wrote, a prince ought to embrace just those policies most popular among the people—leave them to live their lives in peace, not confiscate their property, and so on. Wrote Machiavelli, "The best fortress is to be found in the love of the people."

But a sentiment like that fails to account for how he wound up in the dictionary, whereas this vintage Machiavelli does: A prince "must have a mind disposed to adapt itself according to the wind, and as the variations of fortune dictate, and…not deviate from what is good, if possible, but be able to do evil if constrained." ❖

# The Devil's Dictionary

*By Ambrose Bierce*
*First published in 1906*

Babbits, boosters, flacks and other purveyors of a sunny view of the human condition will find little to sustain them in Ambrose Bierce's misanthropic tour de force, *The Devil's Dictionary*. Why, just turn to the A's and find:

*Air, n. A nutritious substance supplied by a bountiful Providence for the fattening of the poor.*

Proceed to the Z's and encounter:

*Zeal, n. A certain nervous disorder afflicting the young and inexperienced. A passion that goeth before a sprawl.*

This irreverent literary frolic offers welcome respite to the curmudgeon who's spent a vexing day batting off vapidly smiling young waiters and retail clerks determined to wish him a nice day. Marriage, according to Bierce, consists of "a master, a mistress and two slaves, making in all, two." To pray, says the author, means "to ask that the laws of the universe be annulled in behalf of a single petitioner confessedly unworthy." But of course.

Born in 1842, Bierce came out of the Civil War with a distinguished service record in the Union Army and went on to a career as short story writer and journalist. In 1913, at the age of seventy-one, he left for Mexico, presumably to join Pancho Villa's revolutionary army. He was never heard from again.

In *The Devil's Dictionary* (originally *The Cynic's Wordbook*), Bierce leaves us with a taste of our species that is sour at best. But to those not inclined to take him too seriously, and willing to forgive his more outrageous ethnic slurs, his legacy will seem more charmingly eccentric than darkly evil. Sometimes he makes you snicker, sometimes laugh outright; sometimes he embarrasses you with the truth of his insights.

Bierce feels under no compunction to offer each of his thousand or so definitions in the same form. Some, for instance, are epigrammatic, as:

*Positive, adj. Mistaken at the top of one's voice.*

Some definitions amount to brief, barbed essays, as in a disquisition on the word "inadmissible" which argues that the world's religions are all based on evidence inadmissible in any court, while many of history's horrors, like the trial, conviction, and execution of witches, were "sound in logic and in law."

Bierce illustrates other definitions through imagined bits of doggerel by imagined poets and imagined names—Orphea Bowen, say, or Lavatar Shunk. Or Hassan Brubuddy, who adorns this definition:

*Famous, adj. Conspicuously miserable.*

with this verse:

*Done to a turn on the iron, behold*
*Him who to be famous aspired.*
*Content? Well, his grill has a plating of gold.*
*And his twistings are greatly admired.*

Other verses, meanwhile, are lengthier, such as one, accompanying the entry for "a male," that begins:

*The Maker, at Creation's birth,*
*With living things had stocked the earth.*
*From elephants to bats and snails,*
*They all were good, for all were males.*

Or Bierce will treat us to fictional dialogues—like one, between an insurance agent and a homeowner, illuminating his definition of "insurance," which he pictures as a "game of chance in which the player is permitted to enjoy the comfortable conviction that he is beating the man who keeps the table."

Snide? You bet.

Funny? Quietly.

True? That, also. ❖

# Mein Kampf

*By Adolf Hitler*
*First published in 1925*

Hitler, wrote his translator in a note to an American edition of *Mein Kampf*, seldom pursues any logic inherent in the subject matter. He makes the most extraordinary allegations without so much as an attempt to prove them. Often there is no visible connection between one paragraph and the next...His style is without color and movement.

True enough, but would any other author be so excoriated by his own translator? To the modern mind, Hitler has become such a symbol of hatred and cruelty, so much the incarnation of evil, that even normal editorial courtesies are, in his case, suspended. It has become difficult to see him as human, much less the formulator of ideas or the author of a book.

Hitler wrote *Mein Kampf* ("My Struggle") while in prison, after his abortive *putsch* of November 1923. It is, all at once, political manifesto, historical treatise, propaganda manual, autobiography, and an account of the origins of National Socialism, the whole salted with raw hate.

What, exactly, does Hitler say? As artless and crude as his style is, he is not ambiguous, if only because he repeats himself.

He says that it wasn't battlefield ineptitude that led to German defeat in the Great War and the ignominious surrender terms of the Treaty of Versailles; it was a stab in the back delivered by the Marxists and the Jews.

He pictures "The Aryan" as culture creator, "The Jew" as culture destroyer; for Hitler, race, not economics, is at the core of national life.

He extols the spoken word, not the written, for reaching the masses (and regularly recounts his successes in doing so).

He equates a nation's strength with its territory, in effect setting forth a policy of national conquest.

He devalues intellect, holds up physical strength, obedience, and "will" as more essential to the new Aryan man.

He calls for culling out the weak and the infirm from Germany's racial stock.

Mainly, Hitler hates. He hates Jews, parliamentarians, freemasons, the liberal press, Marxists, Social Democrats. He displays open contempt for democratic processes, for intellectual "objectivity," for the masses he proposes to lead, and for any of his followers inclined to take a more accommodating, less bloody road to power.

One does not read *Mein Kampf* today for its political or racial theories, or as a contribution to human thought, or for pleasure. One reads it as a reminder: Tempting though it might be to see Hitler as a once-in-a-millennium aberration, and hence outside the human pale, he was not. He was, truly, one of us; he had a mother and father. He wavered, as most adolescents do, over choice of vocation. Before he was *Der Fuehrer*, he was a penniless painter, trying to make a go of it in prewar Vienna. He was a common soldier. He had youthful dreams, convictions, ideas.

And, at the age of thirty-four, he wrote a book, an uncommonly frank one at that, in which he spelled them all out:

♦ The National Socialist state "must not let itself be confused by the drivel about so-called 'freedom of the press.'"

♦ "The great masses of the people in the very bottom of their hearts tend to be corrupted rather than consciously and purposely evil...Therefore in view of the primitive simplicity of their minds, they more easily fall victim to a big lie than to a little one."

◆ "The future of a movement is conditioned by the fanaticism, yes, the intolerance, with which its adherents uphold it as the sole correct movement."

◆ The National Socialist "movement is antiparliamentarian, and even its participation in a parliamentary institution can only imply activity for its destruction, for eliminating an institution in which we must see one of the gravest symptoms of mankind's decay."

◆ And always the primitive, pornographic anti-Semitism: "With satanic joy in his face, the black-haired Jewish youth lurks in wait for the unsuspecting [Aryan] girl whom he defiles with his blood, thus stealing her from her people."

Vicious, evil, whacko stuff? Sure, but in 1933 Hitler was made chancellor of Germany and legally came to power. ❖

# *Nana*

*By Émile Zola*
*First published in 1880*

Nana is a man-eater, a French courtesan of the glittering Second Empire who gives herself to counts, bankers, actors, boys and men with equal abandon, worms into their psyches only to devour them, robbing them of their dignity and their riches. Capricious, unthinkingly cruel, she is the sexual monster every Parisian man desires; at her house in the Avenue de Villiers, they literally line up outside her bedroom. Her flesh offers delight, her soul corruption.

*Nana* takes place in the same Paris, in the days leading up to the Franco-Prussian War of 1870, immortalized by the French Impressionist school of painting. In the big racetrack scene, Nana cheers a horse named Nana, while the Comte Xavier de Vandeuvres, one of her sexual slaves, tries to recreate his Nana-decimated fortune through a rigged betting scheme...And all the while bright bonnets and gay, colorful dresses shimmer in the sun, straight out of Degas.

The reader realizes from the first, though, that this is no comedy of manners, no polite, pretty look at Parisian high society: "The rumbling of carriages stopped short, doors slammed, and people entered in little groups, waiting at the barrier before climbing the double staircase behind, where the women, their hips swaying, lingered for the moment." Carriages rumbling, doors slamming, hips swaying: All of *Nana* is like that—rough and gritty, devoid of delicacy. The novel begins with the premier of a new show, *The Blonde Venus*. Someone starts to congratulate the theater owner: "Your theater..." He shoots back: "You mean my brothel."

Nana is a vulgar creature of low estate, a product of Paris's seedy Goutte-d'Or district—a fact of which Zola repeatedly reminds us.

For while *Nana* stands by itself as a novel, it was but part of a twenty-novel saga, written over twenty-two years, collectively called *The Rougon-Macquarts: The Natural and Social History of a Family under the Second Empire.* In it, Zola assumes the role of scientist, bent on methodically portraying through fiction the effects of heredity and environment on one multi-branched family. Nana, needless to say, is from the bastard side, the Macquarts.

Her fortunes follow wild gyrations, from gutter to chateau and back again. We see her first on stage, as the Blonde Venus; she can neither act nor sing, but her stage presence is awesome, at least in the nude. She rises to become the toast of the Parisian demi-monde, but sinks to street-walking. Always the sexual vulture, she preys on the men of Paris—save only for one interlude of genuine passion, when she falls for an actor.

She is not the stereotypical prostitute with the heart of gold. But she is not unremittingly evil, either. She can yell and scream and cruelly taunt, yet in the next breath, seeing her victim suffer, coo him back to glad-heartedness.

Throughout *Nana*, grotesque contrasts abound—the glow of French society against the moral putrefaction underneath. No one exemplifies this better than Muffat, the Catholically upright count, enormously wealthy, chamberlain in the Emperor's court, who is only too glad to be led around with a leash by Nana—toward novel's end almost literally so. Indeed, virtually all the characters in *Nana* are obsessed in one way or another, some by the Church, some by gold, some by spectacle, most all by women's flesh.

*Nana* has its defects. Among them is table conversation that sometimes drags interminably. And if one of the novel's strengths is Zola's raw view of the underside of French society, with all its vulgarity and seediness, that is its weakness, too—that no character is granted a noble sentiment, that all that seems fresh and pure, in all this sordidness, is Nana's magnificent young body. ❖

# Ten Days That Shook the World

*By John Reed*
*First published in 1919*

"My sympathies were not neutral," John Reed admits in the preface
to *Ten Days That Shook the World*, his firsthand account of the Bolshevik
Revolution of 1917. In these pages, foes of the Bolsheviks emerge as
stubborn impediments to the onrushing tide of history while Lenin,
Trotsky and their proletarian partisans are held up as noble representatives of a higher humanity, aglow with a sense of historical mission.

Some critics complained, as did the *London Times*, that Reed had
"swallowed the Bolshevists' propaganda en bloc." Yet others lauded him,
in the words of one, for a "restraint which practically vacuum-cleans the
book of any mere rhetorical passages." Seen against a swirl of contradictory contentions that the Bolshevik Revolution meant the Millennium, on
the one hand, or the Apocalypse, on the other, John Reed's work can
indeed be considered "restrained." For while he made plain his sympathies, he was enough of a reporter to record facts, and to represent views
at odds with his own.

The Harvard-educated Reed, in fact, was considered one of the
crack reporters of his day. Fresh from chronicling the 1917 Mexican civil
war, he went to Russia where, earlier that year, the czar had been over-
thrown and a provisional government under moderate socialist Kerensky
installed. All the while, the Great War raged. While its armies suffered in
the trenches and food ran short in its cities, Russia trembled with the
choice of just what sort of a revolution it wanted, teetering this way or that
with each report from the front or shift in the bread supply.

A tactical dispute as early as 1903 had split Marxists into two factions—the Mensheviks, or minority wing, and the more radical

Bolsheviks, or majority. Fourteen years later, these groups, along with a confusing welter of other parties, struggled for power in the streets and assembly halls of Petrograd and Moscow. Reed was there to record it.

The scene: The Petrograd Soviet, the hub of revolutionary ferment, following the overthrow of the Provisional Government. It "was tenser than ever...The same running men in the dark corridors, squads of workers with rifles, leaders with bulging portfolios arguing, explaining, giving orders as they hurried anxiously along, surrounded by friends and lieutenants. Men literally out of themselves, living prodigies of sleeplessness and work—men unshaven, filthy, with burning eyes who drive upon their fixed purpose full speed on engines of exaltation."

Lenin: "A short, stocky figure, with a big head set down on his shoulders, wide generous mouth, and heavy chin...Unimpressive, to be the idol of a mob loved and revered as perhaps few leaders in history have been. A strange, popular leader—a leader purely by virtue of intellect; colorless, humorless, uncompromising and detached."

Yet Lenin, Trotsky and the others appear here more as political stick figures, uttering pronouncements and advancing lines of argument, than as fully drawn personalities. The events Reed reported from Russia were, after all, primarily political—debates, proclamations, party caucuses, negotiations. And like politics in more staid settings, the tugging back and forth for Russia's destiny often grew tedious.

Reed makes little effort to spare us the dreary details. Two early chapters supply historical grounding. And a prefatory "Notes and Explanations" section guides us through the committees, councils, unions, and cooperatives that was Russia in 1917; the conscientious reader finds himself repeatedly flipping back to learn that the Vikzhel was the influential railway workers' union, or that the Maximalists were an offshoot of the Socialist Revolutionary Party.

None of this, let it be said, is artfully handled. A more sophisticated narrative might have let Reed introduce names and groups only as needed, and to better sift the wheat of historical significance from the chaff of only transiently relevant detail.

Of course, this is not history, but journalism. We hear the Duma in debate, read the latest poster from the Committee for Salvation, stand amidst the tumultuous crowds in the Petrograd Soviet as Lenin lambastes the Mensheviks. *Ten Days* may be all it could be, and even all its author intended. Yet the best part of a century after the event, readers may want something more. They may miss precisely the kind of insight that only history, and the distance of years, can grant. ❖

# Native Son

*By Richard Wright*
*First published in 1940*

It's hard to imagine a less appealing character than Bigger Thomas, a twenty-year-old black ne'er-do-well from the Chicago slums who murders the daughter of his high-minded white employer, decapitates her and stuffs her body into a coal furnace. Later, he literally beats the brains out of his girlfriend with a brick and throws her down the air shaft of an abandoned building in which he is hiding from police.

Bigger is the creation of Richard Wright, a novelist hailed as "the most impressive literary talent yet produced by Negro America," born on a Mississippi plantation in 1901. "The day *Native Son* appeared," wrote critic Irving Howe, "American culture was changed forever." Wright dares to deliver his powerful social message not through a warm, sympathetic victim of injustice, but a "victim" who, by every outward sign, is a brutal killer bereft of human feeling. Understand Bigger Thomas as the harvest of pervasive racial oppression, Wright so much as says, and the black condition in America generally can likewise be understood.

*Native Son* is not stylistically elegant. Like its central character, it is brutal, nervous and crude. Some of its scenes verge on melodrama, and its concluding pages, where a brilliant left-wing lawyer makes Bigger's case before the jury, reads less like novel than social polemic. But the book's overall effect is so shattering, its point of view so relentlessly etched into the reader's consciousness, that it leaves its mark as indelibly today as when it was written almost sixty years ago.

As demonstrated by the nearly fifty translations and foreign editions appearing in the wake of its first printing, *Native Son*'s significance *was* widely recognized then. While rightly decrying it for melodramatic and propagandistic excesses, one critic after another admitted these were more than outweighed by its sheer power. The book was frequently compared to Dostoyevsky's *Crime and Punishment*. And, again, to Theodore Dreiser: "*Native Son* does for the Negro," wrote Clifton Fadiman in the *New Yorker*, "what Theodore Dreiser in *An American Tragedy* did a decade and a half ago for the bewildered, inarticulate American white. The two books are similar in theme, in technique, in their almost paralyzing effect on the reader, and in the large, brooding humanity, quite remote from special pleading, that informs them both."

It takes nothing from its significance as social document to report that Wright's book is, as a reading experience, thoroughly engrossing—especially if you go for blood, gore, decapitations, authentic dialect, flight and capture. Compare it to Dostoyevsky and Dreiser all you like, but *Native Son* is, for much of the 396 pages of one of its early Modern Library editions, a real thriller.

"Brrrrrriiiiiiiing! An alarm clock clanged in the dark and silent room," the book opens, and from that to the final working-out of Bigger's relationship to himself, his lawyer and his crime, the book simply won't be put down. As in other thrillers a notch or two down from Olympian literary heights, you sometimes feel manipulated. And all those pages in the close company of psychopathic murderer Bigger Thomas, as he stalks the streets of Chicago killing and running, desperate and fearful, can scarcely be termed enjoyable. Still, *Native Son* is one classic you never feel you're dutifully slogging through.

For all the antiquity of its slang, for all its dated cast of characters—the red-baiting police chief, the "Front Page" era reporters, the left-wing do-gooder, the aristocratic racist—you come away feeling immersed in a world as current as the morning paper. True, the years have wrought changes, from *Brown vs. Board of Education* and Black Power to Martin Luther King, Jr. and an ever-growing black middle class. Yet *Native Son* remains sadly applicable to at least one slice of black experience—and to white understanding of it. Yes, it's hard to imagine any novelist creating the likes of Bigger Thomas today; but that's because the novelistic challenge Wright tackled first has been taken up by many other writers since, and *not* because of any dearth of true-life models from which to draw. Bigger Thomas is alive and running scared in the run-down black ghettos of every American city. And just as persistent are the conditions which spawned him.

Richard Wright never "defends" Bigger, never justifies his crime; he explains it, but does not explain it away. He says, in effect, "What do you expect?" Subject an entire race first to slavery and then to economic colonialism, pack them together under desperate conditions, deprive them of their human dignity, and Bigger Thomas is the more-than-occasional result: As stimulus breeds response, and oppression breeds crime, so do three centuries of racism breed Bigger Thomas. ❖

# THREE

# Books that Shaped the Western World

| | |
|---|---|
| *Essays* | Michel de Montaigne |
| *The Dialogues* | Plato |
| *The Wealth of Nations* | Adam Smith |
| *An Essay on the Principle of Population* | Thomas Malthus |
| *The Decline and Fall of the Roman Empire* | Edward Gibbon |
| *The Origin of Species* | Charles Darwin |
| *The Histories* | Herodotus |
| *The Federalist Papers* | Hamilton, Madison, Jay |
| *The Annals of Imperial Rome* | Tacitus |
| *The Peloponnesian War* | Thucydides |
| *Democracy in America* | Alexis de Tocqueville |

Why be surprised when these tomes, ostensibly shapers of Western thought and among those products of the human intellect most worth reading and rereading, prove to be just that? Not all are easy. But after two hundred or two thousand years, they amply repay any extra effort they require. In Herodotus, we meet the first historian. In *The Federalist Papers*, Hamilton, Madison, and Jay virtually think a nation into being. Darwin and Adam Smith advance some of the most powerful ideas of the past two centuries. And Montaigne? He is the brother and friend a lot of us wish we had.

# Essays

### By Michel de Montaigne
### First appeared in 1580

"This is the only book in the world of its kind, and its plan is both wild and extravagant," wrote Michel de Montaigne of his *Essays*.

What he meant was, first, that he was himself their subject. And second, that instead of following a line of lockstep logic to some single end, he chose instead to let his thoughts float freely where they wished, however hesitant or contradictory the results might be.

He begins one essay, for example, by distinguishing between goodness and virtue, the first being natural and effortless, the second difficult to achieve; he comments on how—even in his day!—the words goodness and innocence had taken on a tinge of contempt; he notes an Italian's assessment of the soldierly qualities of the French, Spanish, Germans, and Swiss; he tells of how he abhors most of the more brutal vices—but that had he been born with "a more unruly temperament," he'd have likely yielded to them: "I have never observed any great firmness in my soul," he writes, "that would be capable of resisting even the mildest of passions." He goes on to offer a glimpse at his own sex life; gives graphic descriptions of the kinds of torture and execution prevalent in his day—pointing out that whatever cannibals might do is less barbarous by far. And he closes with a comment on man's relationship to animals: "I am not ashamed to admit," he says, "that I cannot easily refuse my dog when he offers to play with me." Grand conclusion to all this? None.

The essay, as a literary form, is Montaigne's legacy. In French, *essai* means a trial or experiment, and that's just how this sixteenth-century humanist saw it—as a tentative, questioning, poking-around into this or that subject: "Of the hundred parts and aspects that each thing has, I take one, sometimes merely licking it, sometimes scraping its surface, and sometimes pinching it to the bone...Since I scatter a word here and a word there, samples torn from their piece and separated without plan or promise, I am not bound to answer for them...I am free to give myself up to doubt and uncertainty."

Montaigne is said to have learned Latin before French, and his essays are studded with quotations from Plutarch, Cicero, Seneca, and others of the classics. Indeed, the essays started out as little more than their author's notes on books he'd read—made necessary, he reveals, by a memory so bad he often forgot what he'd read or, when he did manage to remember, his impressions of it. Later in life, he retired from a legal career to the family estate in southern France, there to think and write on every conceivable subject—on books, lying, the education of children, friendship, the art of conversation...With time, the essays became more intimate, more revealing. Collectively, they amount to an autobiography.

Montaigne, on encountering difficult passages in a book: "I do not bite my nails over them; after making one or two attempts I give them up...What I do not see immediately, I see even less by persisting. Without lightness, I achieve nothing; application and over-serious effort confuse, depress, and weary my brain."

On smells: "If I touch [my mustache] with my gloves or my handkerchief, it holds the scent for the whole day. It betrays the place where I have been. The close, luscious, greedy, long-drawn kisses of youth would adhere to it in the old days, and would remain for several hours afterwards."

Women may sometimes feel offended by Monsieur Montaigne: "Those undisciplined appetites and perverse tastes that they display during their pregnancies are present in their hearts at all times," he writes. It is not the only instance when, in commenting on women, he seems irretrievably locked into his age.

But more often, he reaches across the centuries, with perfect meaning and relevance to our lives today. For he is preoccupied not with some sterile philosophical question but simply on what it means to live well. In that pursuit, he is a tireless questioner, never satisfied that he's gotten to the bottom of things, never willing to toss off too-easy explanations. He is ever fresh.

The *Essays* of Montaigne are a pleasure to read. Montaigne, the man, is a pleasure to meet. ❖

# The Dialogues

### By Plato
### Written in the fourth century B.C.

In 399 B.C. Socrates was condemned to death by an Athenian court. With his friends gathered around him, he carried out the order by drinking from a cup of hemlock, his body growing gradually colder and stiffer as the poison worked. "This was the end of our comrade," as his disciple Plato recorded it, "a man...of all then living we had ever met, the noblest and the wisest and the most just."

Plato was twenty-nine at the time. And in a series of two dozen works written over the rest of his life, he set down the ideas of his master as well as—it is a blurring that scholars still dispute—his own. These, collectively, are known as *The Dialogues*.

It was not the first time men (women didn't figure much in the intellectual life of ancient Greece) had inquired into truth, goodness, and immortality. But in *The Dialogues* such themes get a treatment they do nowhere else. This is not some Great Mind earnestly setting down his beliefs, or expounding a dogma, or issuing a manifesto. Rather, Socrates and his friends meet at the agora and follow, through a process of merciless questioning, a line of argument to its seemingly inevitable conclusion. The "Socratic Method," as we call it today, is not truth itself, but a means of pursuing truth. And it is probably more central to Western thought than any of the particular ideas Socrates held.

In one dialogue, Socrates presses a passing boy into service as a sort of intellectual guinea pig. Watch, he tells a friend, demonstrating his method, "I do nothing but ask questions and give no instruction. Look out if you find me teaching and explaining to him, instead of asking for his opinions."

But isn't intellectual debate often just an exercise in frustration? And isn't the embrace of an idea, only to have it dashed, apt to lead to an abandonment of the search for truth? Such experiences can, Socrates admits to Phaidon, lead people to think that "there is nothing sound and wholesome either in practical affairs or in arguments." But such people are victims, in the same way the misanthrope is a victim of having too often been taken in by would-be friends. Ultimately, "he hates everybody, and believes there is no soundness in anyone at all."

"Don't let us be 'misologues,' hating argument as misanthropes hate men," Socrates cautions Phaidon. "It would be a pitiable disease when there is an argument true and sound...and [that one should] deprive himself of the truth."

As for the subjects of the *Dialogues*, they are many and varied. In the *Meno*, Socrates argues that "virtue," the Greek notion of moral excellence, comes through divine dispensation, and cannot be taught.

Similarly, in the *Ion*, he maintains that the gifts of the poet come through God, not human artistry.

In the *Phaedo*, he considers the nature of the soul, and speculates about the after-world.

Some of the reasoning is intricate, requiring work the casual reader may not want to give it. But much of it, though "philosophical," is accessible, and demands only common sense, readerly attention, and an appreciation for the pleasures of rhetoric.

That truth can be gained through unaided reason, enriched by only minimal contact with the world around us, is a cornerstone of the Socratic method. And this flies in the face of modern science, for example, which stresses a constant checking of reason and logic against nature—a looking-out orientation rather than a looking-within. In the *Phaedo*, Socrates reports on his youthful interest in "natural philosophy," which today we call science. A sterile business, says he. Can anyone believe, he asks his friends, that how our bones and sinews are connected, say, really furnishes the "cause of how we live, or why we act as we do?"

As one or another of Socrates' intellectual combatants fails to raise a seemingly natural objection, the modern reader may feel inclined to jump in with, "But Socrates, isn't it true that...?" In the *Crito,* for example, Socrates concludes he must resist importunings to flee Athens rather than take the hemlock, because it would undermine justice. For a justice-seeker like himself, he says, it would be like being an athlete with a crippled body; his would be a life unworthy of life.

But does cooperating with a corrupt legal system, one might ask, truly serve justice? And could Socrates not accomplish more good by remaining alive? And isn't the life-wish a gift from God, and oughtn't that be honored? Valid or not, and quite aside from how Socrates might answer them, such questions are just the sort *The Dialogues* invite. ❖

## An Inquiry into the Nature and Causes of
# The Wealth of Nations

*By Adam Smith*
*First published in 1776*

The story unfolds in a pin factory in eighteenth-century Britain. There, one man draws out the wire. Another straightens it, a third cuts it, a fourth points it, and so on through eighteen distinct operations. An unskilled worker on his own "could scarce, perhaps, with his utmost industry, make one pin in a day, and certainly could not," we are told, "make twenty." Yet this primitive factory, manned by just ten workers, produces forty-eight thousand pins a day. By multiplying production, we learn, division of labor accounts for "that universal opulence which extends itself to the lower ranks of the people."

The observer of this phenomenon was Adam Smith, professor of moral philosophy at the University of Glasgow, tutor to a duke, and commissioner of customs for the city of Edinburgh. The year was 1776, and as one political columnist has put it, the book he wrote helped "make the modern world."

*An Inquiry into the Nature and Causes of the Wealth of Nations* can be reckoned the founding document of the economic doctrine known as laissez-faire—the notion that the maximum good is done when free men and women meet in a free market to conduct their business unencumbered by government rules, regulations and restraints; laissez-faire is French for "let 'em do it."

The division of labor from which so many benefits flow, Smith wrote, is a natural consequence of "a certain propensity in human nature...to truck, barter and exchange one thing for another." When people can do so freely, prices fall to their lowest level, supplies of scarce goods are fairly apportioned, and even the most menial workers manage to eke out a living. And all this good comes not from any human inclination to do good, but as a natural consequence of actors on a great economic stage pursuing their own ends.

A conservative economist, writing in the 1950s, cautioned that readers should not expect to find in *The Wealth of Nations* an understanding of modern economics. "Reading Smith," wrote Ludwig von Mises, "is no more a substitute for studying economics than reading Euclid is for the study of mathematics." The advice is sound; it was a different world that Smith inhabited.

It was a world before the Industrial Revolution had expanded the scale of enterprise and power. It was a world predating the "service economy," where people actually made things and raised crops, instead of pushing paper and manipulating information. It was a world where, in America at least, labor was in such short supply that a widow with four grown children was a hot marriage prospect. And it was a remarkably stable world—one where the wages paid soldiers were exactly as they'd been 150 years before, and where the prices of some commodities had remained constant for half a century.

All the more remarkable, then, that so many of Smith's insights apply today. He writes, for example, that "philosophers, or men of speculation, whose trade it is not to do anything, but to observe everything," are just as inclined to a division of labor as workers in a pin factory; hence the academic departmentalization of today's university and the narrow specialties of our scientific research.

Smith even comments on the old nature vs. environment debate. The difference between "a philosopher and a common street porter...seems to arise not so much from nature, as from habit, custom and education," he writes. Though perhaps similarly endowed at birth, the two are pointed down very different paths. In time, whatever "difference of talents ...widens by degrees, till at last the vanity of the philosopher is willing to acknowledge scarce any resemblance."

Despite his links to a laissez-faire outlook that leaves workers at the mercy of impersonal market forces, this is not the only time Smith seems to sympathize with them. During Smith's day, workers labored under "combination laws" that barred them from forming trade unions or going out on strike. Ideally, worker and master negotiated as between free equals, Smith felt. But he was hardly blind to the reality of it. "It is not...difficult to foresee which of the two parties must, upon all ordinary occasions, have the advantage," he wrote, citing the combination laws and the employer's superior resources. "Masters," he wrote, "are always and everywhere in a sort of tacit, but constant and uniform combination" to keep wages down. And sometimes even "to sink the wages of labor" through agreements "conducted with the utmost silence and secrecy."

Some things never change. Then, as now, men were moved to buy and sell by the same impulse to personal gain, and greed. And it is for insight into this uncanny constancy of human nature that we read Adam Smith today. ❖

ROBERT KANIGEL

# *An Essay on the Principle of Population*

*By Thomas Malthus*
*First published in 1798*

Men and women are consigned to bleak subsistence, because population, left unchecked, grows faster than the food supply needed to feed them.

This is the essential "Malthusian" idea—and yet it does not quite represent Thomas Malthus fairly. For in the inevitable and unremitting human desperation it suggests, it lays the stress, I think, in a way he never intended. The English philosopher and critic Anthony Flew was right when he said that "what Malthus himself actually advocated differs in important ways from what has become associated with his name."

A clue to how Malthus became intellectual history's Gloomy Gus may lie in his famous essay's full title: "On the Principle of Population as it Affects the Future Improvement of Society, with Remarks on the Speculations of Mr. Godwin, M. Condorcet, and other Writers."

Condorcet was the author of *A History of the Progress of the Human Spirit*, which has been called "the most sublimely confident book...ever written." It declared, among other things, that "there is no limit set to the perfecting of the powers of man; that human perfectibility is in reality indefinite."

Meanwhile, Godwin—who like his French counterpart was aflame with the new utopian ideas coming out of the French Revolution—envisioned a society in which "there will be no war, no crimes, no administration of justice, as it is called, and no government. Besides this, there will be neither disease, anguish, melancholy, nor resentment. Every man will seek, with ineffable ardor, the good of all."

Well, then, set against such sentiments as these, Malthus may indeed be reckoned a reactionary, a negativist, an apologist for the misery and injustice in the world—but only against such a backdrop.

In fact, Malthus's essay is full of brighter visions and cheerier insights. At one point, he outlines a hierarchy of human needs similar to that advanced by modern psychologists of the humanistic school. At another, he denies the inferiority of sensual pleasures as compared to intellectual, cautioning only moderation in their enjoyment. ("Intemperance," he writes, "defeats its own purpose. A walk in the finest day through the most beautiful country, if pursued too far, ends in pain and fatigue.")

Malthus does point out that nature's "infinite variety" includes a darker side. But this, he writes, gives "spirit, life, and prominence to her exuberant beauties, and those roughnesses and inequalities, those inferior parts that support the superior, though they sometimes offend the fastidious microscopic eye of short-sighted man, contribute to the symmetry, grace, and fair proportion of the whole."

Are these the bilious outpourings of a misanthrope?

Malthus argues that the lower classes are doomed to bare subsistence. But he leaves open the possibility that future generations might be beneficiaries of more leisure, better education, and "better and more equal laws."

He argues against the "poor laws" of the time; he thought that though benevolently conceived, they did more harm than good—that they were, to the very people they were supposed to help, "grating, inconvenient, and tyrannical."

Malthus's seeming acceptance of—and even justification for—human misery comes across as, at worst, tough-minded realism. He is hardly the perpetrator of the "vile, infamous theory, [the] revolting blasphemy against nature and mankind," that Marx's collaborator Friedrich Engels placed at his door.

To be sure, Malthus was often just plain wrong. He ridiculed, for example, Condorcet's idea for a system that eerily foreshadows our Social Security. And he pooh-poohed Condorcet's equally prescient vision of longer lifespans and "the gradual removal of transmissible and contagious disorders by the improvement of physical knowledge."

But wrong or not, Malthus advanced his views and countered those of his foes with rare intellectual vigor. That may explain, even more than those views themselves, why from the beginning they excited such fierce opposition—and why today they are remembered.

Godwin's utopia would ultimately lead to a time, Malthus wrote, when "the spirit of benevolence, cherished and invigorated by plenty, is repressed by the chilling breath of want...The corn plucked before it is ripe, or secreted in unfair proportions, and the whole black train of vices that belong to falsehood are immediately generated. Provisions no longer flow in for the support of the mother with a large family. The children are sickly from insufficient food. The rosy flush of health gives place to the pallid cheek and hollow eye of misery. Benevolence, yet lingering in a few bosoms, makes some faint expiring struggles, till at length self-love resumes his wonted empire and lords it triumphant over the world."

A "Malthusian nightmare" if ever there was one. ❖

# The Decline and Fall of the Roman Empire

*By Edward Gibbon*
*First published in six volumes between 1776 and 1788*

"It was at Rome, on the fifteenth of October, 1764, as I sat musing amidst the ruins of the Capitol, while the barefooted friars were singing vespers in the Temple of Jupiter, that the idea of writing the decline and fall of the city first started to my mind."

When the great project was finished twenty-four years later, it encompassed the whole Roman Empire and spanned a period from the emperor Marcus Aurelius in the second century A.D. to the fall of Constantinople in 1452.

The first of Gibbon's six-volume history, while warmly received by the public, incurred the wrath of clerics and scholars. For Gibbon had dared explain the rise of Christianity paralleling Rome's decline, largely in human terms. Oh, the correctness of Christian doctrine, Gibbon had dutifully noted, was of course the primary reason for its success. But as "the wisdom of Providence frequently condescends to use the passions of the human heart...to execute its purpose," he had accordingly explored these secondary causes.

This fiction fooled no one. For the "secondary" causes included the Machiavellian intrigues of popes and bishops, the rapaciousness of the crusaders, the zealotry of monks and martyrs, and the like. Unlikely to endear Gibbon to the church, for example, was his observation that monks capable of inflicting pain upon themselves in pursuit of spiritual purity rarely felt much "lively affection for the rest of mankind. A cruel, unfeeling temper has distinguished the monks of every age and country: their stern indifference, which is seldom mollified by personal friendship, is inflamed by religious hatred."

Plainly, then, Gibbon's monumental work is no dreary listing of dates, kings, and battles. Despite its great length, it rarely bogs down in tiresome detail; Gibbon has already done the selecting, has plucked from his great reservoir of scholarship only those facts that illuminate his point, relying on the telling detail, not every detail. His is the story of early Western civilization distilled and digested by a clear mind—and a heart alive to history's victims.

At one point, while telling how the pure and simple faith of the early Christians ultimately degenerated into worship of saints and relics, Gibbon relates how relics of St. Stephen had been instrumental in the swift conversion of 540 Jews. Of course, he adds, this was achieved "with the help, indeed, of some wholesome severities, such as burning the synagogue, driving the obstinate infidels to starve among the rocks, etc."

Gibbon brought to his task vast scholarship, calm reason never twisted by prejudice, and gentle irony. He also brought formidable expository skills—as in his description, for example, of the new city of Constantinople, established by the Emperor Constantine in the fourth century A.D. and capital of the eastern, or Byzantine, branch of the Roman Empire for the next thousand years. Gibbon transports us there, where Europe and Asia meet, to see "the winding channel though which the waters of the Euxine flow with a rapid and incessant course towards the Mediterranean."

Modern readers will find Gibbon's insights into human nature as applicable to today's events as to the fall of Rome. For example, Gibbon tells how the early church tended to attract sinners of every stripe, while those of more moderate temperament stayed away. Writes he: "Those persons who in the world had followed, though in an imperfect manner, the dictates of benevolence and propriety, derived such a calm satisfaction from the opinion of their own rectitude as rendered them much less susceptible of the sudden emotions of shame, of grief, and of terror, which have given birth to so many wonderful conversions." To those passing from sin into the welcoming embrace of the church, "the desire of perfection became the ruling passion of their soul; and it is well known that while reason embraces a cold mediocrity, our passions hurry us with rapid violence over the space which lies between the most opposite extremes."

By virtue of its length and awesome historical sweep, *The Decline and Fall of the Roman Empire* has become a metaphor for all those literary works of weight and substance that one sets aside for a time of future leisure but, presumably, never reads. It is, indeed, substantial; the numerous abridgements available make it more manageable. And yet, so tasty is Gibbon that even, say, a four-hundred-page appetizer is apt to leave one hungry for the whole meal.

Gibbon elsewhere records that he composed in whole paragraphs, often staying his pen from the page while his thoughts percolated, forming and reforming in his mind. What emerged were elegant sentences promenading up and down the page that leave you wanting more—more of his delicious irony, more of his gentlemanly calm, more of the stately grandeur of his prose. ❖

# The Origin of Species
## By Means of Natural Selection,
## Or the Preservation of Favored Races in the Struggle for Life

*By Charles Darwin*
*First published in 1859*

When H. L. Mencken went south to Tennessee in 1925 to attend the circus that was the "monkey trial," it was Charles Darwin up on the stand as much as the schoolteacher John Scopes. Scopes had dared teach evolution, Darwin's theory that higher forms of life were descended from lower forms, and the whole weight of southern fundamentalism was arrayed against him.

Today, the trial of Darwin's ideas continues. His name still crops up often in debates of social policy and scientific theory. Schoolbook controversies in several states have pitted a new, and more sophisticated, crop of "creationist" thinkers against today's prevailing view that evolution is more than theory, but sure and certain scientific fact.

And it all began with *The Origin of Species*. Here are all the catch phrases that have pulled at the public imagination for a century: Survival of the fittest, the struggle for existence, natural selection. All that's missing is the famous monkey to which man is presumably tied by common ancestry. (He makes his appearance in Darwin's sequel, *The Descent of Man*.)

The idea of evolution wasn't all that new in 1859; Europe had flirted with it for a century. "Survival of the fittest" was not Darwin's phrase but Herbert Spencer's. And another scientist, Alfred Russel Wallace, was around the same time reaching conclusions almost identical to his. Yet in large part thanks to the massive evidence he offered, the product of twenty years of study, it is Darwin we remember today.

All organisms, wrote Darwin, are locked in a struggle for scarce food, water, and safety—for life itself. Any slight hereditary variation giving one individual a better shot at survival may be passed on to its progeny. A longer-legged gazelle, to use a classic example of Darwin's popularizers, is better fitted to outrun the lion, reproduce itself, and so pass on its genetic superiority; its shorter-legged cousins, meanwhile, are more apt to die out. Thus, a new species may arise through what Darwin called "natural selection."

Darwin's readers, we should recall, were abundantly familiar with *human* selection. If man could create new and specialized breeds of roses or pigeons in the space of a few generations, how many more could Nature create, over the eons? So went one of the book's key lines of argument.

Darwin himself softened his emphasis on natural selection in later editions of the book. And scientists to come, in particular De Vries, would offer "mutations"—large abrupt changes rather than slight, successive ones—to account for the origin of new species. Still, the core of Darwin's idea remains compelling, and influential beyond measure, to the present day.

Darwin called his work "one long argument," which it is, marching inexorably onward, tackling objections, assembling new proof at every turn. Throughout, one is reminded of how great scientific leaps lie grounded in the masses of routine observation that precede them: Darwin everywhere credits unremembered scientists—A. de Chandolle's study of oak trees, and B.D. Walsh's entomological studies, for example—with leading him to the raw data on which his conclusions are based.

Unlike most of today's scientific works, *The Origin of Species* leaves scant distance between the theory being advanced and the man advancing it. Chapter six begins: "Long before the reader has arrived at this part of my work, a crowd of difficulties will have occurred to him. Some of them are so serious that to this day I can hardly reflect on them without being in some degree staggered." Most, he insists, are "only apparent," and the rest are "not fatal to the theory." In any case, we are left with a vision of Darwin himself, as if a too-small boy, beset by detractors and enemies, "staggering" under the weight of his argument.

Many readers, it should be said, will find Darwin tough going, and may turn to more popular recapitulations of his ideas. (Jacques Barzun has termed *The Origin of Species* "one of those ideal books, like Marx's *Capital*, that need not be read to be talked about.") Though occasionally reaching for dramatic flourishes, his style is convoluted, and the book's scientific base will make it hard slogging for many.

On the other hand, Darwin is never cold to the natural world he aims to describe. Amidst all the recital of fact and marshaling of argument shines something of the mystic's sense of wonder at the sheer diversity of the universe. And nowhere is it more evident than in the book's concluding paragraphs:

"It is interesting," writes Darwin, "to contemplate a tangled bank, clothed with many plants of many kinds, with birds singing on the bushes, with various insects flitting about, and with worms crawling through the damp earth, and to reflect that these elaborately constructed forms, so different from each other, and dependent upon each other in so complex a manner, have all been produced by laws. Thus, from the war of nature, from famine and death, the most exalted object which we are capable of conceiving, namely the production of the higher animals, directly follows.

"There is grandeur in this view of life, with its several powers, having been originally breathed by the Creator into a few forms or into one; and that, whilst this planet has gone cycling on according to the fixed law of gravity, from so simple a beginning endless forms most beautiful and most wonderful have been, and are being, evolved." ❖

# The Histories

*By Herodotus*
*Written in the fifth century B.C.*

Astyages, king of Scythia in the sixth century B.C., dreams of a vine that grows from his daughter's genitals and spreads over Asia. His pregnant daughter's son will usurp the throne, he's warned. So he orders a trusted lieutenant, Harpagus, to kill the infant.

Harpagus can't do it himself, but gives the child to a herdsman, instructing him to leave the infant exposed in the wild, mountainous country he inhabits. But the herdsman's wife convinces her husband to show Harpagus her own child's body, just delivered stillborn, as evidence of their compliance with his orders—and to bring up the king's grandson as their own.

The ruse works. The boy lives. But at about age ten, circumstances bring him to the attention of Astyages, who guesses the boy's identity, and resolves to punish his lieutenant. "Since things have taken this lucky turn," he tells Harpagus, "I want you to send your own son to visit the young newcomer, and come to dinner with me yourself."

That evening they feast. Assured that Harpagus has had his fill, Astyages orders his men to serve him a final covered platter—the head, hands and feet of Harpagus' son, whom Astyages has had butchered and on whom Harpagus has just dined. Thus does the king exact his revenge.

The story is vintage Herodotus, all the ingredients in place: blood and gore, dreams and oracles, scheming and intrigue and sheer human drama.

Herodotus was born in what is now Turkey in the fifth century B.C. In *The Histories*, the one work for which he is known 2,500 years later, his subject is the struggle between the emerging Greek city-states and the mighty Persian Empire. But interwoven in the chronological account are endless digressions. We learn about the flooding of the Nile and its effects on agriculture, about the construction of the pyramids, about the nomadic ways of the Scythian tribes, about the crystal coffins of the Ethiopians. We hear of political options discussed, plots hatched, dreams interpreted, battles fought.

Of course, not all of it is strictly true; that Herodotus has heard a story is, by his lights, reason enough to tell it. He records that when certain Indians mined gold, they had to do so quickly, lest they be caught by ants bigger than foxes. And that Arabs stole cinnamon from the large birds who used it for their nests. How? By feeding them dead oxen and donkeys in chunks so large their nests crumbled from the weight, scattering the cinnamon to the ground.

In Herodotus's time, the boundaries between myth, superstition, legend, prophesy and what we today too confidently term "fact" were blurrier than they are now. But even then, it's plain, Herodotus knew he was telling some tall ones. Sometimes, he'd let a whopper slip by without any disclaimer—a failing that has contributed to his being known as the Father of Lies as well as the Father of History. More typically, he'd tell the story, then add that he couldn't swear it was true, or even admit its unlikelihood. But let the story's seeming lack of veracity bar its telling? Never.

For that we can be grateful on several counts. First, had Herodotus too scrupulously clung to sure and certain fact, our insight into the mind of the fifth century B.C. would be immeasurably poorer. Second, his narrative wouldn't have been such fun to read. Third, some stories Herodotus dismissed as impossible—for example, that the Nile has its source in melting snows—proved true.

Herodotus tells how among the Scythians, a nomadic race inhabiting what is today's Ukraine, it was the custom among the men to drink the blood of the first man they killed in battle; and that bringing a head to the

Constitution's various provisions and tackle the arguments against it. They make appeals to historical precedent, invoke philosophers from Plato to Montesquieu, and employ every rhetorical device, freely resorting to analogy and metaphor when logic and fact fail.

At one point, Madison tries to make us sympathize with the formidable difficulties the framers faced in simply marking off the line between the state and federal roles. So he likens their task to that faced by, of all people, naturalists—whose attempts to mark off the various forms of animals and vegetable life are likewise fraught with difficulty.

It's a commonplace today to declare our leaders not of the intellectual stature of those of yore. Nostalgia-fogged sentiment? Maybe so, but one need go no further than *The Federalist Papers* to sympathize with the assertion. The most able of our time turn to science, business, or the arts —much less so to politics. Who today boasts the insight into human nature, the sheer force of intellect, that Hamilton and Madison reveal in these essays?

The Constitution that has so successfully piloted the country through wars, insurrections, attacks on its legitimacy, and various crises of corruption was, *The Federalist Papers* remind us, thought out beforehand. The framers anticipated problems, foresaw human excesses and moral shortcomings. They carefully, deliberately built in that intricate system of controls that generations of Civics I students have learned to parrot back as "checks-and-balances."

If our government was designed, the Constitution was its blueprint. But unlike a bridge or other engineering structure, which need cope only with predictable forces and known stresses, our republic was designed to withstand largely unpredictable forces induced by human passions, needs and drives.

It is not too much to linger on this technical analogy. The American Revolution, after all, was a product of the Enlightenment, that eighteenth-century intellectual movement that saw reason as the one sure route to human betterment. *The Federalist Papers* pulse with its spirit. The political means the new Constitution would employ, Hamilton writes, were "wholly new discoveries," the consequence of a much advanced "science of politics." For him, the virtues of representative government, checks and balances and all the rest had been demonstrated through historical *experiment.*

Government's task was nothing less than to transcend human nature. Human beings, the authors say on every page, are quick to anger, slow to think; they segregate into factions, try to gather power to themselves, deny it to others. "So strong is the propensity of mankind to fall into mutual animosities," writes Hamilton, "that where no substantial occasion presents itself the most frivolous and fanciful distinctions have been sufficient to kindle their unfriendly passions and excite their most violent conflicts." Property holders contend with the propertyless, farmers with manufacturers. "The passions of men will not conform to the dictates of reason and justice without constraint," he goes on. Little is to be gained by imagining they will; better to design around the human material.

So it's no accident we have a government that's so ably weathered crises, panics, wars and other expressions of human folly; it was designed that way. ❖

# The Annals of Imperial Rome

*By Tacitus*
*First appeared circa 100 A.D.*

When Christ was born, Augustus ruled the Roman Empire. After a forty-five-year reign, he died, and power passed to the morose and cunning Tiberius, his adopted son; twenty-three years later to mad, murderous Caligula; then to the seemingly weak-minded Claudius; and then to Nero—who may not have fiddled while Rome burned but rather sung. While Roman legions subdued tribal revolts in Germany, Britain and throughout the Mediterranean, the capital was engulfed in political turmoil, intrigue, sexual excess, and murders performed by every means men and women could conceive.

From a perch removed by half a century from all the madness, cruelty and blood, Tacitus chronicled the history of this crucial period, one that helped sow the seeds of modern Europe. His account comes down to us (after a 1,400-year period before the Renaissance, when it went largely ignored) as *The Annals of Imperial Rome*. Originally covering the years 14 to 68 A.D., the surviving *Annals* contain gaps, most notably the brief but bloody reign of Caligula.

Tacitus chronicled the lives and fortunes of his highborn subjects, but also commented upon them with relish and bite. As one critic has observed, "Even the most inept and donnish translators have never been able to erase it." The Senate's noisy mourning for Tiberius' son Drusus, writes Tacitus, was "insincere and unconvincing." Charges brought against a certain official were downright "preposterous."

This is no faceless history by a recorder bound to canons of strict, pseudoscientific objectivity. Tacitus himself is always right there, launching into digressions, commenting upon this conspirator's character flaws, that emperor's hidden motivations. Not that he imposes his own reading on events; indeed, in several instances, he takes care to offer variant interpretations. But he's not inclined, either, to let a choice incident go without comment when he can just as well pass judgment with a sneer.

Sometimes just such a biting writerly presence is needed to relieve the tedium of plots, poisonings, suicides and miscellaneous bloodlettings —a tedium of which Tacitus himself is aware. At one point, contrasting his own history with those of an earlier, more illustrious span of Rome's past, he admits: "My themes...concern cruel orders, unremitting accusations, treacherous friendships, innocent men ruined—a conspicuously monotonous glut of downfalls and their monotonous causes." And the sheer, unrelenting human baseness he reveals does sometimes pall; one yearns for a hero to stand up for what he believes, and to worry about someone's skin besides his own.

How much does all this grim business simply reflect the times (perhaps, as Tacitus writes, a sign of "heaven's anger with Rome")? How much owes to Tacitus' sneering stance? And more, an English-speaking reader is apt to wonder, how much is an artifact of translation? The style of Tacitus' Latin, after all, has been described as "idiosyncratic," and "the despair of the translator."

One translator, Michael Grant, gives this reading of Tacitus: It was the final days of Claudius' reign and "Agrippina had long decided on murder. Now she saw her opportunity. Her agents were ready. But she needed advice about poisons." In a prefatory note to his translation, Grant observes that the best way to render Tacitus into English is through "as pungent a simplicity as the translator can achieve."

Compare Grant's with this other translation of the same passage: "It was then that Agrippina, long since bent upon the impious deed, and eagerly seizing the present occasion, well-furnished as she was with wicked agents, deliberated upon the nature of the poison she would use." Pungent simplicity it lacks. And yet, though mired in polysyllables, it bears much the same acerbity as Grant's.

*That* is Tacitus. And something in the Imperial Rome of the first century brought it out in him. ❖

# The Peloponnesian War

*By Thucydides*
*Written circa 404 B.C.*

The time: the fifth century B.C., soon after the outbreak of the long, bloody conflict between Athens and Sparta known today as the Peloponnesian War. Athens, at the height of its power and influence, is burying its war dead. Following custom, their bones have been returned to the city, and Pericles, Athens' gifted leader, has been asked to address the mourners. In a rhetorical master-stroke, he barely mentions the dead. Instead—and with an eye toward future battles as much as past—he praises the city for which they fell.

Our Athens, he says, is a democracy, its form of government a model to others. In it, power goes to the capable, not the well-connected, and poverty is no bar to public service. Our people are tolerant of others, yet respectful of the law, which "commands our deep respect."

But not all is seriousness. "When our work is over, we are in a position to enjoy all kinds of recreations for our spirits...In our homes we find a beauty and good taste which delight us every day and which drive away our cares."

Lest this seem self-indulgent, he goes on, "our love of what is beautiful does not lead to extravagance; our love of the things of the mind does not make us soft. We regard wealth as something to be properly used, rather than as something to boast about..."

On and on goes this litany of Athenian virtue. Delivered ostensibly in praise of the dead, Pericles' funeral oration is actually civics lesson, patriotic appeal, moralistic entreaty and call to arms all in one. "This," concludes Pericles, "is the kind of city for which these men, who could not bear the thought of losing her, nobly fought and nobly died." This, he reminds his audience, is what they must defend.

Whether Pericles, who died two years later in the plague that dev-astated Athens, said every word attributed to him is unclear. In form, Thucydides' history of the war is a straightforward account of battles and troop movements punctuated by the texts of speeches marking decisive moments in the conflict: Should the Plateans be put to death for failing to aid Sparta? Do the Mytilenians, who have revolted against Athens, deserve Spartan support? Yet Thucydides confesses that neither he nor his informants always recalled the precise wording of key speeches. And so, he explains, "while keeping as closely as possible to the general sense of the words that were actually used," he has endeavored "to make the speakers say what, in my opinion, was called for by each situation."

Contradictory? Perhaps. But except in the most narrowly literal sense, it hardly matters. These ideas and sentiments plainly *could* have been expressed. Whether Thucydides expressed them—or Pericles or Alcibiades or Cleon—they suggest what the Greeks thought worth saying. Their logic is, mostly, compelling. They are laced with appeals to human nature, self-interest, and common sense.

Perhaps three-quarters of the book records the movements of sol-diers and ships, battlefield geography, the numbers and arms of opposing forces, the ebb and flow of battle, who died, who didn't, what revenge was exacted on the losers, and so on. Even in this day of laser-guided missiles, generals will draw lessons. Those of unmilitary bent, meanwhile, will find these accounts appealing to the imagination as human drama, and to the intellect as puzzles: *How can we dislodge the Spartans from that rocky island at Pylos?*

During a break in the siege of Pylos, Spartan emissaries go to Athens and appeal for peace. Don't be greedy, they say. You have the upper hand now, but who knows how things will go? Let's put our mutual enmity behind us; do not impose terms too vengeful. For "no lasting set-tlement can be made in a spirit of revenge, when one side gets the better of things in war and forces its opponent to swear to carry out the terms of an unequal treaty." Those who imposed on Germany the harsh Treaty of Versailles, which ended the First World War but planted the seeds of the Second, plainly never read their Thucydides

During a revolution, Thucydides observes, words lose their meaning. "What used to be described as a thoughtless act of aggression was now regarded as the courage one would expect to find in a party member...Fanatical enthusiasm was the mark of a real man...Anyone who held violent opinions could always be trusted, and anyone who objected to them became a suspect."

Is this Corcyra in the wake of its civil war in 427 B.C.? Or France during the Reign of Terror of 1793? Or our world, wracked by spasms of terrorist violence, today? ❖

# Democracy in America

*By Alexis de Tocqueville*
*First published in 1835*

What gifts of perception and intellect equip one to meet a callow teenager and predict his personality, quirks and all, as an old man? Whatever they are, Alexis de Tocqueville had them. The "teenager" was America of the early 1830s, when Thomas Jefferson was dead barely five years. America today, a century and a half older, its arteries clogged with the detritus of history, can only marvel at the precision of Tocqueville's insights.

The son of a French aristocrat, Tocqueville came to America in 1831, stayed nine months, traveled seven thousand miles. His ostensible purpose? To study the American penal system. In fact, nothing about America, its institutions or its people, escaped his fresh eye and penetrating intelligence. He returned to France in the late winter of 1832, and soon set to work on what would be his enduring classic, *Democracy in America*, published in two volumes, in 1835 and 1840. To this day no book about the American national character is so often, and so profitably, quoted.

America is something new, says Toqueville—the most advanced expression of a universal and irresistible human urge to break down the old feudalism and all its rigid class distinctions. "I saw in America more than America," he tells his readers in an introduction. "It was the shape of democracy itself which I sought, its inclinations, character, prejudices and passions; I wanted to understand it so as at least to know what we [in Europe] have to fear or hope."

He is not American democracy's unalloyed admirer. There is, first of all, the maddening mediocrity that seems to flourish on our shores. And a lowering of the level of intellectual debate to that below what a Parisian could expect in any sidewalk cafe. And a "tyranny of the majority" that leaves little room for originality of either thought or opinion.

But overshadowing these defects are, among other things, American respect for laws; American democracy's tendency toward slow, peaceful change; the difficulty faced by evil-doers in controlling enough levers of power to do harm; and a narrowing of extremes of wealth.

Though disquisitions on lawmaking and other such textbook staples occupy their share of it, *Democracy in America* will interest not only students of history and government; virtually every aspect of the American national character swings into focus under Tocqueville's microscope, from race relations, to the family, to religion, to manners, to the arts.

Occasionally, as when he sees Americans as little more than transplanted Englishmen (without benefit of immigrant cross-fertilization), or when he pictures Americans as unlikely to make major advances in theoretical science, he is revealed as merely human. For an instant, the reader may actually feel miffed, only to abruptly realize he's so disappointed Tocqueville is wrong only because Tocqueville is right so astoundingly often.

Tocqueville describes Americans as people whose lives are "so practical, so confused, so excited, so active, that little time remains for them for thought."

He says of democratic institutions that they "awaken and foster a passion for equality which they can never satisfy." He could be describing Edison as well as the Apollo moon project when he says that "in America, the purely practical side of science is cultivated admirably... The Americans always display a clear, free, original and creative turn of mind."

Tocqueville even anticipates mass production. In a democracy, the people's desire for goods "outrun[s] their means and [they] will gladly agree to put up with an imperfect substitute rather than do without the object of their desire altogether..." One solution "is to find better, quicker, more skillful ways of making it. The second is to make a great number of objects which are more or less the same but not so good..."

It would be the best part of a century before the first Model T came rolling off Henry Ford's assembly line. ❖

# Making Hard Work Easy

### The Great Popularizers

| | |
|---|---|
| *Only Yesterday* | Frederick Lewis Allen |
| *Microbe Hunters* | Paul de Kruif |
| *Selected Works* | Cicero |
| *Coming of Age in Samoa* | Margaret Mead |
| *The Outermost House* | Henry Beston |
| *The Amiable Baltimoreans* | Francis F. Beirne |
| *What to Listen for in Music* | Aaron Copland |
| *Gods, Graves, and Scholars* | C. W. Ceram |
| *The Stress of Life* | Hans Selye |
| *The Greek Way* | Edith Hamilton |

---

To some, "popularization" verges on a dirty word. A recent cartoon shows one elderly scholar saying to another, "At least, we haven't stooped to popularizing." Even when not condemned outright, popularization normally carries little cachet, is rarely seen as a nonfiction genre in the way that science fiction, say, ranks as a distinct, if lesser, fictional one.

But it takes talent to bring an inchoate mass of arcane material to life. A new generation of writers has made "popular science" something like its own genre. But not only science benefits from the popularizing impulse; so do history, anthropology, music. And as we see here, some of the best examples of it long predate the current crop.

# Only Yesterday
## An Informal History of the 1920s

*By Frederick Lewis Allen*
*First published in 1931*

On October 24, 1929, in the offices of J. P. Morgan & Company, reporters eagerly awaited the words of Thomas W. Lamont, a representative of the mighty financial house. Lamont looked grave. "There has been," he said, "a little distress selling on the Stock Exchange."

October 24 was the first panicky selling day of the Crash of '29. In the first two hours of trading, United States Steel dropped twelve dollars a share. Montgomery Ward plummeted from eighty-three to fifty. Dozens of stocks lost all they had gained in the preceding months of the bull market.

That was Thursday. Monday brought even more precipitous declines. Then came Black Tuesday, when the bottom dropped out of the market altogether and panic reached its heights: With a scream of financial agony, the Roaring Twenties were over.

Today our image of the tumultuous Twenties is apt to be colored by nostalgia, distorted by TV and movies, or simply dimmed by ignorance. To us it was the heyday of our parents or grandparents' generation. In 1931, on the other hand, when Frederick Lewis Allen wrote his "informal history" of the decade, the Twenties were still "only yesterday."

At the end of World War I, the country was exhausted. It craved what the next president, Warren Harding, would call "normalcy." America wanted to keep out foreigners and kick out Reds; both were European, alien, and dangerous. It wanted nothing so much as to be left alone to play, and to make money. The Ku Klux Klan was resurgent, its membership reaching 4.5 million by 1924. Bolsheviks and those suspected of sympathizing with them were rounded up on a scale worthy of the McCarthy era three decades later.

Meanwhile, hemlines rose. Women stopped hiding behind Victorian bustles. Sex and Freud became the stuff of dinner party conversation. Automobiles, and automobile culture, spread across the land. Prohibition brought speakeasies, and hip flasks, and Al Capone's beer trucks roaring across Chicago—and Al Capone's thugs shooting up anyone who tried to get in the way.

And everywhere—except on the depressed farms—big bucks were being made. By Florida real estate developers. By publicists for the waves of stunt fliers who followed in the wake of Lindbergh's heroic solo Atlantic crossing. And by everyone, or so it seemed, on the Stock Exchange, where it was buy, buy, buy, and still the chattering ticker tape in your local broker's office told the tale of fortunes to be made, always and forever, world without end.

Until finally the great, overstretched balloon of American prosperity burst.

The stock market collapsed. Consumers stopped buying. Factories stopped producing. Workers stopped working. The ballyhoo days were over. The world became a more serious place.

The same financiers who in the Twenties had offered their pronouncements as gods, had no answers for the unemployed of the Thirties. The need, Allen writes with prescience, was for someone wise enough to know what to do and strong enough to get the chance to do it. The name of Franklin D. Roosevelt appears nowhere, not even parenthetically, in Allen's account.

Everything had happened so fast, the face of America was transformed overnight. How could Allen make sense of it, from a distance in time offering such meager perspective, while the country was still immersed in a terrible Depression whose end was not yet in sight? That he did, somehow, is *Only Yesterday*'s triumph.

It would be like writing, in 1971, a history of the 1960s—surely no one would take the trouble to write one of the 1970s—with the national mind still reeling from hippies and acid trips and assassinations and Black Power and the insanity of Vietnam. No one has done it, even now, not the way Allen did with the Twenties. This is one measure of his achievement.

Another is that while *Only Yesterday* mostly remains as fresh and immediate as when it was written, its interpretations have stood the test of more than half a century. In his introduction to a 1957 edition of the book, one critic, Roger Butterfield, wrote, reasonably enough: "It is time to say what has long been apparent—that this is an American classic." ❖

# Microbe Hunters

*By Paul de Kruif*
*First published in 1926*

Among the pioneers of medical research Paul de Kruif portrays in *Microbe Hunters*, none are soulless technicians, gray accountants of dreary fact, or objective seekers after truth unmoved by visions of glory; de Kruif thus makes short work of some of the more common stereotypes about scientists.

But not all—not, for example, that of the Mad Scientist: Most of the author's microbe hunters are, in fact, just a bit daft.

Not certifiably insane, maybe, but surely driven, arrogant, and obsessed. Preoccupied with their scientific quests, they'll go to any lengths for The Answer. Their persistence is pathological, as is their confidence: Emil Behring, in search of a cure for diphtheria, fairly massacres whole herds of guinea pigs. Louis Pasteur, fearfully protective of his achievements, responds to an attack on his theories, writes de Kruif, with a paper whose arguments "could not have fooled the jury of a county debating society."

Some years ago, Tracy Kidder won a Pulitzer Prize for *The Soul of a New Machine*, an intimate behind-the-scenes look at the frenzied development of a new computer and the impassioned men who did it. For many people, bits and bytes and silicon chips make up a world overwhelmingly alien and gray; but Kidder pictured it as burning with a white heat of intellectual and personal ferment. He reported the gritty dailiness of the work as much as the high drama; yet, for all that, it was a romanticized portrayal. Romanticization, it seems, is an occupational hazard of the genre, a genre whose prototype is, by any measure, *Microbe Hunters*.

"This plain history would not be complete if I were not to make a confession," de Kruif writes on its final page. "I love these microbe hunters, from old Antony Leeuwenhoek [inventor of the microscope] to Paul Ehrlich [discoverer of a syphillis cure]. Not especially for the discoveries they have made nor for the boons they have brought mankind. No. I love them for the men they are."

De Kruif finds his subjects full of grievous flaws: Antony Leeuwenhoek is sadly unimaginative, failing to guess that the microbes he sees under his microscope bear disease. Koch, who discovered the tuberculosis bacillus, is a cold technician cursed, to pathological excess, with German thoroughness. Louis Pasteur is an arrogant showman, impossibly rash and sloppy. But none of this detracts from de Kruif's awe of his subjects; rather, it humanizes them—and helps to forge intense reader interest. The author could doubtless fashion a story of Attila the Hun that recounted every particular of his savagery, yet managed to "humanize" him.

De Kruif's fierce attachment to his subjects mirrors that of the scientists themselves for their work. Pasteur, his theories questioned by posthumously published research, rises indignantly on the floor of the French Academy of Medicine to denounce his enemies, then runs off to perform the exquisite experiment that proves him right after all.

Elie Metchnikoff, a morphine addict inclined to periodic suicide attempts, goes off to Sicily with his young bride. There, he examines starfish larvae under the microscope, sees microscopic organisms eating other microscopic organisms—and gives the rest of his scientific life over to the holy grail of the "phagocytes" he's discovered and named, and the immunity to disease they confer.

De Kruif's prose, it must be said, too often degenerates into an effervescent cutesiness. Vexatious, too, are certain mannerisms of style and certain pet phrases—like "wee beasts" and "little animals" to describe microorganisms, and words like "gorgeous" to describe an elegant experiment, or "stuff" for a microbial stew. For de Kruif, "flashes of lightning" are forever marking the scientist's way.

But such stage-lit prose arises from the author's wish to illuminate dramatically a terrain that might otherwise be mistaken for being stark, alien, and gray. De Kruif knows it's not. When he describes experiments (and he does so with impressive clarity), we await their outcome with real eagerness. We are there as Ehrlich finds his "magic bullet"…as Lazzaro Spallanzani conceives a way to isolate a single microorganism and then, under the microscope, sees it split in two before him.

"Two hundred and fifty years ago an obscure man named Leeuwenhoek looked for the first time into a mysterious new world peopled with a thousand different kinds of tiny beings, some ferocious and deadly, others friendly and useful, many of them more important to mankind than any continent or archipelago."

Thus, with the stylistic excess that is its hallmark, *Microbe Hunters* begins.

But doesn't it make you want to read it? ❖

# Selected Works

*By Marcus Tullius Cicero*
*First appeared between 60 and 44 B.C.*

Must an orator possess wide knowledge of many fields? Or can he simply collect odd scraps of information as needed and weave them, through his skill, into a spellbinding oration?

One day in 91 B.C., leading orators of the day met at a villa in Tusculum outside Rome to ponder that question. Crassus, the foremost public speaker of his time, was there. So was his friend Marcus Antonius, grandfather of the Mark Antony of "Friends, Romans, countrymen..." fame, and a speaker known for his easy, seemingly offhand delivery. Their debate, in the presence of younger colleagues, comes down to us today in Cicero's "On the Orator."

In those days, orators were regarded more highly than they are today, when we are apt to dismiss them as demagogic manipulators of people and language. At the time of the Roman republic, however, the orator was seen more as statesman than politician. And Cicero, a contemporary (and foe) of Julius Caesar, defender of Rome against the Catiline conspiracy, was the most distinguished master of Latin prose of all. For him, the art of the orator was beyond all others.

Could one master it without mastering the whole of human knowledge? No, Cicero has Crassus saying, "Unless the speaker grasps and understands what he is talking about, his speech will be worthless." Not so, replies Antonius; mastery of specialized knowledge is "entirely unconnected with the proper function and business of an orator."

In fact, Antonius never said any such thing. Nor did he, Crassus, and the others meet at Tusculum that day in 91 B.C. Rather, the semi-fictional gathering was Cicero's way of making accessible a subject otherwise abstract and difficult. In other writings, Cicero applied the same device to consider, for example, friendship ("Laelius") and moral goodness ("Discussions at Tusculum").

Cicero was himself no heavyweight thinker. But he was a good enough middle-weight to enjoy the intellectual company of the Greek philosophers of three centuries before. In effect, he translated the classical Greek mind, for which philosophy was as natural as breathing, into terms the Roman mind, for which it was not, could understand. He was a popularizer, and a measure of his success is that students of the classics have learned much of what they know about Greek thought through him.

But Cicero's popularizing bent is weakness as well as strength. For one senses that this is picked-over intellectual territory—as indeed it was by the first century before Christ. The ideas are no longer spontaneous, raw, and unfinished. Rather, it's as if Cicero had catalogued the main lines of thought that had come down to him, smoothed over the sharp edges and assembled them all in a neat package, like a college outline.

Of course it's all charmingly done. Cicero was no noisy ideologue, convinced of the rightness of his views and the wrongness of all others. Rather, he was of genuinely eclectic temperament, at home with all ideas, wedded to none, committed only to their free interplay: Antonius demolishes the views of his opponent, Crassus, but only after paying homage to them.

At one point, the two speak gratefully of at last being free of the press of public business and having time for matters of the intellect. Who today, one wonders, derives such delight in employing leisure so profitably? ❖

# Coming of Age in Samoa
## A Psychological Study of Primitive Youth for Western Civilization

*By Margaret Mead*
*First published in 1928*

Back in 1925, before jet planes shrank the world, it took the young Margaret Mead two weeks to reach her island in the south Pacific. The twenty-three-year-old anthropologist remained on Tau, in the Manu'a archipelago, for nine months, closely observing village life, in particular that of its girls and young women.

Then, in 1928, appeared *Coming of Age in Samoa*, the book based on her research, and critics of the day realized it was more than just another dry academic treatise. "Warmly human, yet never sentimental, frank with the clean, clear frankness of the scientist," wrote one. For another, it was "an extraordinarily brilliant and, so far as I am aware, unique piece of work."

What Mead was doing, she explained, was a kind of experiment, using the natural laboratory furnished by a primitive island culture: Were the *sturm und drang* of the teenage years, their nervousness, tumult, and rebellion, inevitable? "Were these difficulties due to being adolescent," Mead wondered, "or to being adolescent in America?" Any society where this familiar teenage pathology was missing, she suggested, would show it was nurture that was responsible, not nature.

But for twelve chapters, as Mead immerses her readers in the life of the island, this overarching question recedes into the background: We rise to the sound of cocks crowing, and to "the insistent roar of the reef." We watch boys going off to fish in their dug-out canoes, girls looking after the smaller children, or weaving mats. We encounter the odd, floating, ever-permeable Samoan household where, faced with even a breath of discontent, one just moves out of one thatched hut and into another. We're treated to a chapter on dance, the one area of island life where excellence is not discouraged in the name of easy getting-along. Finally, after dark, it's "under the palm trees," the indigenous euphemism for clandestine lovers not so clandestinely coupling.

Occasionally, this broad survey of an irresistibly charming culture reads like the anthropology, the science, it is: "Obligations either to give general assistance or to give specific traditionally required service, as in a marriage or at a birth, fellow relationship lines, not household lines." Such detached academic stuff, while *not* typical, suggests that Mead didn't completely bridge the gap to "popular" writing, at least by today's standards.

Then comes Chapter thirteen. Abruptly, what had been merely interesting begins to glow with brilliance. It's as if the author had been holding back, husbanding her energy, like a baseball pitcher lazily warming up before reaching back for the first high, hard one over the plate. "For many chapters," she writes, "we have followed the lives of Samoan girls, watched them change from babies to baby-tenders, learn to make the oven and weave fine mats, forsake the life of the gang to become more active members of the household, defer marriage through as many years of casual love-making as possible, finally marry and settle down to rearing children who will repeat the same cycle."

Now she returns, almost triumphantly, and with liberated energies, to her original question, almost forgotten while we've lolled about the pretty Pacific paradise: *Is the pathology of adolescence inevitable, or just an artifact of Western civilization?* Well, she replies, if her carefree, well-adjusted Samoan girls are any measure, it's *not* inevitable.

Mead observes that the American teenager, unlike the Samoan, is faced with a plethora of choice, which she calls "the forerunner of conflict." In a delightful parody, she imagines an adolescent whose father might be "Presbyterian, an imperialist, a vegetarian, a teetotaler, with a strong literary preference for Edmund Burke, a believer in the open shop and high tariff," and so on—versus other family members whose values and lifestyles differ in every conceivable way from his, and from each other. How, then, is the poor, confused child to pick among them? No wonder she's nervous and tense.

Then, too, Samoa is a more forgiving society than ours, Mead notes—a place where a "low-grade moron would not be hopelessly handicapped," and where those afflicted with "slight nervous instability" can get along just fine.

But these represent just a sample of her insights. The point is, suddenly it's *Western* society that swings under her magnifying lens— nervous, chaotic, furiously paced. Moreover, the three quarters of a century since her work first appeared have left it even more so, the lessons it might draw from the gentle Samoans all the more telling. ❖

ROBERT   KANIGEL

# The Outermost House

*By Henry Beston*
*First published in 1928*

"East and ahead of the coast of North America, some thirty miles
and more from the inner shores of Massachusetts, there stands in the open
Atlantic the last fragment of an ancient and vanished land. For twenty
miles this last and outer earth faces the ever hostile ocean in the form of
a great eroded cliff of earth and clay, the undulations and levels of whose
rim now stand a hundred, now a hundred and fifty feet above the tides.
Worn by the breakers and the rains, disintegrated by the wind, it still
stands bold."

This is Cape Cod, and one September many years ago, the naturalist Henry Beston took up residence there, at its outermost edge, in a
two-room cottage he'd designed and built on Eastham Beach, facing the
North Atlantic. To the south lay only dune. His sole neighbors were coast
guardsmen at the Nauset lighthouse a couple of miles north. Twice a
week, a friend took him into town for groceries. For drinking water, he
drove a well directly down through the sand...There, on that solitary
dune, his little house "faced the four corners of the world." There, Beston
resolved to live a whole year, alone, and record the life of wind, sea,
marsh, and dune he saw there.

*The Outermost House*, Beston's record of that year, has been called
"a classic of American nature writing." In 1964, the Governor of
Massachusetts and other dignitaries met on the Cape Cod beach to dedi-
cate a plaque to the cabin in which it was written. The years since have
seen Outermost House washed away. They have also, I think, weakened
readers' tolerance for the kind of effusively lyrical language in which the
book that bears its name was written.

"The beach at night has a voice all its own," Beston writes, "a sound in fullest harmony with its spirit and mood—with its little dry noise of sand forever moving, with its solemn, overspilling, rhythmic seas, with its eternity of stars that sometimes seem to hang down like a lamp from the high heavens—and that sound the piping of a bird..."

Now this is wonderful stuff, make no mistake. *But the whole book is like that*—rhapsodic, swooning, dripping with nature's beauty; and 222 pages of it, with virtually no retreat to anything plainer, sometimes deflects attention from the natural wonders the author would evoke, and onto itself.

"The world today is sick to its thin blood for lack of elemental things, for fire before the hands, for water welling from the earth, for air, for the dear earth itself underfoot. In my world of beach and dune these elemental presences lived and had their being, and under their arch there moved an incomparable pageant of nature and the year. The flux and reflux of ocean, the incomings of waves, the gatherings of birds, the pilgrimages of the peoples of the sea, winter and storm, the splendour of autumn and the holiness of spring—all these were part of the great beach."

Is there a trace of smugness in all this? Does it read as much like a religious tract, a fervid paean to Nature, as a calm, quiet vision of the natural world? Is the author, like a lovesick teenager, almost *too* consumed by passion? How, one wonders, could so spartan and so elemental a life as Beston lived for a year on that lonely beach produce prose so mannered and overwrought?

*On the other hand*, something in the mad intensity and joy of the author's solitary life is compelling, and, for many readers, that will carry the day. It matters so much to him, we sense—the terns floating overhead, the crickets racing off into the dune grass, the irresistible heaving of the sea—that in the end it matters to us. Maybe it *is* overdone, too full of florid sentiments and alliterative lushness...But he is only a man, a writer, and the ultimate power and truth of the natural world he describes transcends his excesses. So that almost despite himself, Beston wins: He's made you care. ❖

# The Amiable Baltimoreans

*By Francis F. Beirne*
*First published in 1951*

What makes any city the way it is? What about a city is fixed and immutable? How does it shape its inhabitants? Or is it actually that people shape the cities in which they live? Or perhaps places and people are both merely products of their times?

*The Amiable Baltimoreans*, originally one of a group of volumes about various cities and regions known as the Society in America series, does not set out to provide answers to such questions; less assuming by far, it pretends only to being a light account of Baltimore, its history, its institutions, its personalities. Still, reading it today grants a unique perspective. At almost fifty, it is neither old enough to be of solely historical interest, nor so recent as to render a portrait of the city faithful to today. Rather, it lies on the cusp, offering much that is familiar, yet always as if seen through a gentle time warp.

Many old landmarks are here—Johns Hopkins Hospital and the Preakness, H. L. Mencken and the Mobtown tradition, Fort McHenry and the city's fabled steamed crabs. But so are many no longer familiar—once-prominent stars in the urban constellation now dimmed, important families now forgotten, a skyline unrecognizable.

Such changes are, of course, inevitable with the passage of time and don't, by themselves, give the book its odd, funhouse mirror quality. What does is the author's tone, so alien to today's sensibilities. To Beirne, writing in the early 1950s, a world war just won and America everywhere ascendant, everything seemed certain, assured, under control. Institutions were institutions, history was history. Class, racial, and gender distinctions were givens. The manifold democratizations ushered in by the 1960s, with the dissolution of so many rock-solid certainties, lay in the future.

Beirne, editor and columnist with a local newspaper now extinct, could still comfortably describe how the issue of admitting female undergraduates to Johns Hopkins University "solved itself in a most satisfactory manner." By their being admitted? No, that was still most of a century off. Rather, by the establishment of a Woman's College of Baltimore, which became Goucher College. "So young women have not needed to go to the Hopkins for their undergraduate training," Beirne writes approvingly. "Goucher can give them all they need."

Jews are portrayed as "rapidly pushing the old hunting set out of the Green Spring Valley." Does he mean simply that some Jews were buying houses there, or something more? Blacks, still "Negroes" in 1951, had made gratifying progress in gaining their rights, Beirne notes—so gratifying that "There is a tendency for the more radical element to increase its demand with the end to wiping out all racial distinction. This," he added, "is not likely for many years to come."

While Jews and blacks, among the minorities, had by the 1940s already begun to make themselves heard, the ethnic movement had not yet surfaced. So that while we learn of contributions made by German immigrants of the nineteenth century, Beirne has nothing to say of more recent newcomers from eastern and southern Europe—like the Poles and Italians, who already occupied block after rowhouse-dense block of East Baltimore. It is a flabbergasting omission.

Beirne is always the perfect gentleman, charming, quick to put a good face on everything. When his book first appeared, a critic for the *New Yorker* complained that the author apparently felt that "in writing about a city it's not chivalrous to ruffle the sensibilities of anybody who lives there." A badmouther, for example, might label Baltimoreans, as a group, illiterate; Beirne says, rather, that "they do not enjoy a reputation for being bookish." Even when recounting riots and scandals, Beirne seems more amused than shocked or outraged. Everything's fine, each page seems to say. Pain and passion are never much in evidence.

Facts are facts, of course, and Beirne's assembling of them—dolloped out in chapters given over to sports, medicine, theater, society, and the like—is certainly as good as any, and probably more amusing than most. His account of Baltimore's obsession with the weather, particularly the phenomenon of "the two-inch snowstorm," is delightful—and on the mark.

But while facts are facts, history, the lens through which they're viewed, changes with time. So that even aside from any changes that historical research has revealed since 1951, today's reader will find the author's account skewed. For Beirne, society still breaks down into Leaders and Great Figures on the one hand, and everyone else on the other. We don't think that way anymore, or at least don't admit to it. *The Amiable Baltimoreans* takes us back to a seemingly simpler, more ordered, more comprehensible time, when stormy winds of change had scarcely begun to blow—or if they had, were scarcely noticed. ❖

# What to Listen for in Music

*By Aaron Copland*
*First published in 1939*

To fans of Frank Sinatra, or Bruce Springsteen, or Alanis Morissette, lions of the "classical" music tradition like Beethoven and Bach can seem unapproachable. Their music may lack singable melody or danceable beat, be more complex and textured, more ambitious in design. The classical vocabulary, laced with terms like passacaglia, sonata, opus and divertimento, can be alienating. Finally, classical composers have by now become so synonymous with High Culture that "Bach" and "Beethoven" are no longer just men who wrote inspired music but cultural icons whose mere mention can make the uninitiated cower.

Doesn't have to be, said the modern American composer Aaron Copland. In a series of fifteen lectures given in the late 1930s to lay audiences at the New School for Social Research in New York, Copland fashioned a sort of field guide to the flora and fauna of the classical landscape. *What to Listen for in Music* is the written record of those lectures.

Music need not be just a blur of pretty notes, Copland tells us. We listen on several planes at once—on the emotional, on the "expressive" (what does the music "say"?), and on the purely musical. Even the novice can probably tell a Bach fugue from a Tchaikovsky symphony. But what makes them so different? Why do they leave us in such different moods? Why may one come to life only with repeated listening, while the other is instantly accessible?

Copland, who wrote the ballet score for *Appalachian Spring* among other works of note, equips us to find out. He introduces rhythm, melody, harmony and tone color as the basic elements of music; outlines musical texture and structure; surveys musical forms, like theme-and-variations,

# Gods, Graves, and Scholars

*By C. W. Ceram*
*First published in 1951*

In 1917, the English archeologist Howard Carter discovered the tomb of Tutankhamen, an Eighteenth Dynasty Egyptian pharoah who ruled in the fourteenth century B.C....From such a piling-up of names and dates, *Gods, Graves, and Scholars* suffers not at all. Rather, author C. W. Ceram tells how Carter's excitement mounted as the digging for the suspected tomb progressed: "Step after step appeared out of the rubble, and as the sudden Egyptian night closed in, the level of the twelfth step came to light, disclosing 'the upper part of a doorway, blocked, plastered, and sealed...' "

Then, later: "Taking an iron testing rod, Carter poked it through the door and found an emptiness on the other side. He lit candles to ensure against poisonous gases. Then the hole was enlarged.

"Everyone interested in the project now crowded about... Nervously, Carter lit a match, touched it to the candle, and held it toward the hole. As his head neared the opening—he was literally trembling with expectation and curiosity—the warm air escaping from the chamber beyond the door made the candle flare up..."

Much of Ceram's account of archeological discovery is like this— crammed with facts, but also breathless with the same thrill of unraveling the mysteries of a buried past that motivates the great archeologists he chronicles.

The reader is there as the Frenchman Champollion deciphers the Rosetta Stone, key to understanding Egyptian hieroglyphic. He marches with Cortes' conquistadors into the Mexican jungle as they "behead" an advanced Indian civilization that predated their arrival by more than a thousand years. He looks on as Schliemann unearths Homer's fabled Troy and discovers a priceless treasure: "There was the soft sheen of ivory, the jingle of gold. Schliemann's wife held open the shawl to be filled with [what they took to be] Priam's treasure. It was the golden treasure of one of the mightiest kings of prehistory, gathered together in blood and tears, the ornaments of a godlike people, buried for three thousand years until dug from under the ruined walls of seven vanished kingdoms."

Now such wide-eyed wonderment is ripe for sophisticated sneering —on the grounds, for example, that it leaves insufficient room to properly develop a line of thought or body of scholarly knowledge. Indeed, when *Gods, Graves, and Scholars* first appeared, a reviewer for the *New Yorker* complained that it was "cozy and popeyed, and...nearly always skimpy." But that was a discordant note in an otherwise friendly reception. One critic called it "the best popular history of archeology." Another declared that it would "do for archeology what *The Story of Civilization* did to popularize that far less dramatic subject."

Since then, Ceram's book has been translated into twenty-six languages, and repeatedly reprinted. In 1967, it was updated. Those who have read it, or someday will, probably number a thousand times those having read, for example, *Monumenti antichi inediti*, by Johann Joachim Winckelmann, one of the fathers of archeology.

In his preface, Ceram—a pseudonym of journalist Kurt W. Marek —acknowledges a debt to Paul de Kruif, whose *Microbe Hunters* pioneered what Ceram calls the "new literary category" of science popularization. Here lies the key to viewing a book like *Gods, Graves, and Scholars* which is not itself, in a sense, "original": It must be seen by its own lights, not as the sort of scholarly book it was never meant to be, but as part of a distinct genre for which we today have ever more need. ❖

# The Stress of Life

*By Hans Selye*
*First published in 1956*

Loud noise does it. So does extreme cold. Or a burnt finger. Or an intractable math problem. Or a stern lecture from your boss. All impose stress. All can make you sick.

Back in 1925, Viennese-born Hans Selye was a medical student at the University of Prague. His professors paraded before him patients suffering from a variety of infectious diseases, in each case noting the symptoms and little telltale signs that distinguished one from another. But what young Selye noticed was not how different the sick people were, but how alike. Aches and pains, intestinal disturbance, fever—these were common, whatever the particular illness. Together, it seemed to him, they comprised a "syndrome of just being sick."

That perception stuck with him over the years and led to his discovery that the body responded to demands placed upon it with a universal, non-specific response; and that too strong a response could lead to illness, those of the kidneys, heart, and blood vessels being among them.

The story is told in Selye's *The Stress of Life*, first published in 1956, when it was received as, in the words of one reviewer, "an extremely intense and personal book in which the personality of the writer is ever present." Updated in 1976 to reflect two decades of new research, it retains most of Selye's quirky blending of autobiography, scientific discovery, self-help, and philosophy.

Selye first saw the effects of stress in rats he'd injected with various ovarian and placental extracts. Autopsy revealed heightened adrenal activity, shrinkage of the thymus and other immune system organs, and ulcers in the stomach lining. Surely, something in the extract he was injecting had done it. Discovery of some new sex hormone, he felt confident, was just around the corner.

Then, he found he could inject the rats with a toxic substance called formalin and get the same response—only stronger.

Scratch the sex hormone idea. "I do not think I had ever been more profoundly disappointed!" Selye writes. "Suddenly all my dreams of discovering a new hormone were shattered. All the time and all the materials that went into this long study were wasted."

But later he remembered his "syndrome of just being sick" from medical school. Were the symptoms he'd seen in the rats a general response to assault on the body akin to the general syndrome he'd seen back in medical school? He thought they were, and called it the "general adaptation syndrome." His first paper on it appeared in 1936.

Years of research followed, confirming the essentials of his theory and leaving Selye the acknowledged father of a field in which, by the mid-1970s, more than one hundred thousand scientific papers had been written. Selye himself is the author of more than fifteen hundred articles and thirty books. But it's *The Stress of Life* that's brought the stress concept out from the medical libraries and onto the lay public's bookshelf; that's helped make laments about "the stress of modern life" and worry about "all the stress he's under lately" part of popular culture.

What's unusual about Selye's book is its catholicity of form.

It is, first, quite personal. We're there with the young Selye for key experiments, both failed and successful, that led him to the stress concept.

It is also an exercise in science popularization. We learn how an infection, say, triggers release of corticotrophin releasing factor from the hypothalamus, which releases ACTH from the pituitary, which in turn orders the adrenal glands to secrete corticoids, which act on the immune system, and so on. Some readers, despite Selye's best efforts, may find

not thoughts, and that is even truer of Pindar's poetry."

Hamilton takes similar leaps with the great Greek tragedians. Aeschylus evokes the same sense of exalted pain as Shakespeare; so she quotes Macbeth as much as Agamemnon. Sophocles—that "quintessence of the Greek"—reminds her of Milton; she reads a passage from the blind poet and concludes: "It is hard to believe that Sophocles did not write that."

*The Greek Way* sets out with firm and overriding purpose to impress on the modern mind the Greek achievement, and never wanders from it. Hamilton, unworried about nit-picky buts and maybes, sacrifices scholarly nuance. Indeed, when the book came out in 1930, she took her critical lumps for bulldozing important distinctions in her rush to get across the message. *New Statesman* declared that her excesses of enthusiasm would "make the ordinary reader thankful that his son is on the science side at school. The style is that of the direct statement with seventy-five percent of the statements unsupported by documentation."

Such carping, though, was buried in praise for what the book so ably achieved. Wrote one reviewer: "We do not know a book which we prefer to this, if we were asked to recommend an introduction to the peculiar quality of Greek thought which gives it value to ordinary people."

What was that "peculiar quality?" Taking us on a whirlwind tour of other ancient civilizations—India, Rome, Egypt—Hamilton approaches it by contrast to what it was not. The Egyptians, for example, were preoccupied with death, while "Greece resisted and rejoiced and turned full-face to life." The Egyptians built Pyramids and underground burial vaults; the Greeks played. "The Greeks were the first people in the world to play…If we had no other knowledge of what the Greeks were like…the fact that they were in love with play and played magnificently would be proof enough of how they lived and how they looked at life."

Edith Hamilton, who died in 1963, was a world renowned classicist. Born in Dresden, Germany, she grew up in Fort Wayne, Indiana, and served as headmistress of a Baltimore girls school from 1896 to 1922. But her soul was always elsewhere, in the distant past, and far away. On her ninetieth birthday, King Paul of Greece made her an honorary citizen of Athens.

"Five hundred years before Christ in a little town on the far western border of the settled and civilized world, a strange new power was at work." So begins *The Greek Way*.

"Something had awakened in the minds and spirits of the men there which so influenced the world that the slow passage of long time, of century upon century and the shattering changes they brought, would be powerless to wear away that deep impress. Athens had entered upon her brief and magnificent flowering of genius." ❖

# FIVE

# Not Robinson Crusoe, Not Brave New World

## Lesser Known Classics

| | |
|---|---|
| *A Journal of the Plague Year* | Daniel Defoe |
| *The Doors of Perception* | Aldous Huxley |
| *Elective Affinities* | Johann Wolfgang von Goethe |
| *Homage to Catalonia* | George Orwell |
| *Civilization and Its Discontents* | Sigmund Freud |
| *Arrowsmith* | Sinclair Lewis |
| *Roughing It* | Mark Twain |

---

These days, winners and losers split ever further apart. Publishers abjure "midlist" books and concentrate on a few blockbusters. Books, movies, and rock bands must score big, or not at all; "modest success" verges on oxymoron. So today, when we hear Aldous Huxley, we think *Brave New World.* Sinclair Lewis? *Main Street.* Goethe? *Faust.* The selections here, however, remind us that these and other authors wrote more than the one or two books for which they're most famous.

# A Journal of the Plague Year

*By Daniel Defoe*
*First published in 1722*

A leather purse lying in the street bulges with money. For an hour, it lies there, no one drawing near. Finally, one enterprising man scatters some gunpowder over the purse and ignites it, filling the air with heavy smoke. Then, with a pair of tongs, red hot at the tips, he holds the singed purse and shakes free, into a pail of water, the thirteen shillings it contains. Such was the care one took, in the terrible year of 1665, to avoid infection by the plague.

At the height of it, twenty thousand Londoners died in a week. Each night, carts carried off the corpses to pits into which they were flung. During the day, once-thronged streets went largely deserted, quiet except for the wailing cries of the dying and their families locked inside. The whole story is told in *A Journal of the Plague Year* by, as the original title page has it, *a Citizen who continued all the while in London.*

The "citizen" tells of a group of women he finds ransacking an abandoned warehouse, "fitting themselves with hats as unconcerned and quiet as if they had been at a hatter's shop." He tells how a band of Londoners fled the city, squatting in abandoned houses or building rude lean-tos in the countryside, evading by one ruse or another local townsmen who wanted them gone.

He credits the city fathers with never allowing the dead to accumulate on the street. Of course, he adds, they had little trouble recruiting laborers to cart off the corpses, a dangerous and unsavory job, thanks to the many impoverished by the economic desolation wrought by the plague.

From this presumably straightforward account, a vivid picture of its author emerges. He feels compassion for the victims, gratitude that he is not among them, outrage at the frauds and quacks who peddle amulets and cures to the desperate and the unsuspecting. He is slow to condemn those fleeing the city and their responsibilities as physicians or clergy, quick to laud the mayor for insuring an uninterrupted flow of food to the poor. He is a scrupulously careful observer, often qualifying his report with "or so I heard it said" or "I did not see this for myself, but believe it true." And while he fears God, frequently invoking His name, he never succumbs to zealotry. God's will is done well enough through nature's customary workings, he assures us, that we need not invoke supernatural powers.

Of course whether any of this actually describes the man whom history records as the author of *A Journal of the Plague Year*, Daniel Defoe, who also wrote *Robinson Crusoe* and *Moll Flanders,* we do not know. Because Defoe was, in fact, five years old when the plague struck London. *A Journal of the Plague Year* is fiction.

Scholars tell us that Defoe's library was stocked with books like *Necessary Directions for the Preventions and Cure of the Plague* and *London's Dreadful Visitation,* both published in the plague's immediate wake. And while growing up, he certainly heard about it from family, friends and neighbors. In any event, Defoe inspires supreme confidence, and his account is probably at least as true as any with a greater formal claim to historical accuracy.

(Though called a "journal," Defoe's is not a diary or daily account of the kind familiar to us today. Nor is the text divided into chapters. Nor is it broken up in any other way. Instead, the paragraphs arrive without let-up for almost three hundred pages, leaving the modern reader, at least, groping for the work's shape and structure. It is an instructive lesson in the virtues of breaking text into manageable morsels.)

One day, readers learn, the "bills," or weekly death listings, abruptly drop by two thousand over the previous week. "It is impossible to express the change that appeared in the very countenances of the people that Thursday morning when the weekly bill came out," writes Defoe. "A secret surprise and smile of joy sat on everybody's face. They shook one another by the hands in the streets, who would hardly go on the same side of the way with one another before. When the streets were not too broad they would open their windows and call from one house to another, and ask...if they had heard the good news."

Having endured, in these pages, the deaths of a hundred thousand Londoners, the reader can scarcely fail to share the elation and gratitude felt by the survivors; indeed, he may feel like one himself. ❖

# The Doors of Perception

*By Aldous Huxley*
*First published in 1954*

One May morning almost half a century ago, the English novelist, essayist, and critic Aldous Huxley swallowed four tenths of a gram of mescaline, the active ingredient in the hallucinogenic cactus peyote, used ritually by certain Indian tribes, then sat down "to wait for the results."

*The Doors of Perception*—the title is from a line by the poet William Blake—is an account of his experience. "Visions of many-colored geometries, of animated architectures, rich with gems and fabulously lovely, of landscapes with heroic figures, of symbolic dramas trembling perpetually on the verge of the ultimate revelation"—which of these most moved the author? None. They never happened. They are what he *expected* would happen.

It was not his inner universe that Huxley found enriched by the drug but the everyday world around him. "The other world to which mescaline admitted me was not the world of visions," he stresses. "It existed out there, in what I could see with my eyes open."

A small glass vase, for instance, contained three flowers which, under the influence of the drug, fairly popped out at him with primeval life. "I was not looking now at an unusual flower arrangement. I was seeing what Adam had seen on the morning of his creation—the miracle, moment by moment, of naked existence." It was Plato, who had confused original Being with the abstraction of Idea, laments Huxley. He "could never, poor fellow, have seen a bunch of flowers shining with their own inner light."

These intense perceptual experiences lead Huxley to embrace the notion advanced by the French philosopher Bergson, among others—and not at odds with scientific thinking today—that the brain functions as a filter, sieving out excessive and confusing sensory stimuli that would otherwise overwhelm the organism. Under mescaline, he suggests, this nervous system filter is lacking—letting the world rush in with unchecked force, just as it rushes, uncontrollably, into the consciousness of the schizophrenic.

At one point, Huxley observed strong shadows cast across a garden chair. "That chair—shall I ever forget it? Where the shadows fell on the canvas upholstery, stripes of a deep but flowing indigo alternated with stripes of an incandescence so intensely bright that it was hard to believe that they could be made of anything but blue fire…It was inexpressibly wonderful, wonderful to the point, almost, of being terrifying. And suddenly I had an inkling of what it must feel like to be mad."

"So you think you know where madness lies?" asks the scientific investigator at whose suggestion Huxley had tried the drug. He replies, unhesitatingly, "Yes."

Compared to the onrush of sensory color he encounters with mescaline, everyday reality seems gray indeed. Even as glimpsed by artists. Huxley opens a volume of Van Gogh reproductions of "The Chair." Under the influence of the drug, it seems to him a flop. (Would a Van Gogh original, one wonders, have been different?) "Though incomparably more real than the chairs of ordinary perception, the chair in his picture remained no more than an unusually expressive symbol of the fact." The artist had failed to communicate the sheer reality of the chair.

Which leads Huxley to ruminations on Cezanne, Botticelli, Vermeer, the significance of drapery in painting, the ties between Zen and Chinese landscape art…

Aldous Huxley experimented with mescaline ten years before the world had ever heard of LSD or Timothy Leary. He was, at the time, sixty years old, a distinguished man of letters. Indeed, his slim book became a minor classic which, during the subsequent decade, many chose to read as apologia for the drug revolution then raging.

But one need not accept the values of that revolution to read with unflagging interest what this immensely perceptive man, and first class writer, had to say about one afternoon's experience. ❖

# Elective Affinities

*By Johann Wolfgang von Goethe*
*First published in 1809*

A middle-aged married man falls in love with a young girl. His wife is irresistibly drawn to her husband's boyhood chum. Fireworks ensue.

The scene is a lush estate in the German countryside during the time of Napoleon. The man is Eduard, pampered and self-indulgent. His friend is known simply as The Captain. Eduard's wife, Charlotte, is a woman of refined intelligence and uncommon good sense. The object of his infatuation is Ottilie, a quiet, ascetic child who attends the same boarding school as Charlotte's daughter from a previous marriage. Ottilie is all silent mystery, giving what could be a soap opera of a story its haunting power.

As a title, *Elective Affinities* risks reinforcing the stereotype of Germanic abstraction and pedantry. Goethe himself admitted it was strange. The reference, made clear in an early chapter, is to how each chemical substance exhibits its own affinity for other substances, showing up as a greater or lesser tendency to combine or react with them. Thus, as one character explains, the two great classes of compounds known as the acids and alkalis, though "mutually antithetical, and perhaps precisely because they are so, most decidedly seek and embrace one another, modify one another, and together form a new substance."

Lest it be lost that all this may refer to more than chemistry, Charlotte observes, in a foreshadowing of the rest of the story, that the combining substances "possess not so much an affinity of blood as an affinity of mind and soul. It is in just this way that truly meaningful friendships can arise among human beings: for antithetical qualities make possible a closer and more intimate union."

This novel, almost two centuries old, smacks not at all of musty age; its freedom of content and form makes it seem thoroughly modern. Sometimes, in mid-paragraph, the past tense abruptly gives way to the present: "Eduard returns and learns what has happened, he rushes into the room, he throws himself down beside her, clasps her hand and bathes it with silent tears..." The sense is that of stage directions, of critical intellect suspended, leaving only bare action. At other times, an otherwise straightforward account yields to diary entries, letters, even to a brief story-within-a-story reminiscent of those of Doris Lessing in *The Golden Notebook*.

Goethe's world of the German gentry was vastly freer in matters of sex and marriage than anything we associate with the same period in America, which corresponded to Thomas Jefferson's presidency. Divorce was common, unsanctified liaisons not unknown; for eighteen years, Goethe himself "lived together," as we say today, with a younger woman and had five children by her, before marrying her at the age of fifty-seven. Then, two years later, he fell in love with an eighteen-year-old. The ensuing turmoil provided the material for *Elective Affinities*.

In it, the principal characters freely discuss serial marriage. Sexual tension runs at high fever throughout. And a partner-swapping scheme involving divorce and remarriage is the aim of most of the principal players.

In one respect, though, the novel reveals anything but modern sensibilities. Goethe confines his attention to the mansion on the hill and its aristocratic denizens, consigning the hundreds huddled in the town below to obscurity. Inn owners occasionally appear, and servants, and nameless physicians. And for comic relief so does the unforgettable Mittler, who serves as professional mediator, family therapist, and general busybody, quick to intrude at the first sign of domestic trouble. But all these function as so many worker ants, there to satisfy the everyday needs and passing fancies of the gentry. Meanwhile, Charlotte, Eduard and the others celebrate birthdays, indulge their passions, comment intelligently on matters of the heart and the mind, or debate the landscaping merits of one path up the mountain versus another.

Goethe, author of *Faust* and German literature's surest claimant to the mantle of genius, is no spinner of light romances. *Elective Affinities* is a story of both lust and love, of passions silly and grand, of suffering self-indulgent and noble. But for all its echoes of *Bob and Carol and Ted and Alice*, it is not apt to be picked up, consumed, and forgotten. ❖

ROBERT KANIGEL

# Homage to Catalonia

*By George Orwell*
*First published in 1938*


In December 1936, more than ten years before he was to write *1984*, George Orwell went to Spain to report on the civil war between Republican loyalists and insurgent Fascist generals led by Francisco Franco.

This was no ordinary civil war. Spain's popularly elected leftist government drew arms and support from Soviet Russia, while Mussolini and Hitler supplied the Fascists. The war gripped the attention of the world. It excited grand passions. It was impossible to be neutral about it.

Orwell—his real name was Eric Blair—fell under Spain's spell. Stirred by the heady egalitarian spirit of revolutionary Barcelona, the principal city of the region known as Catalonia, he enlisted in a militia unit linked to a Trotskyist political party. For three months he fought in the trenches of the Aragon front. Then he returned to Barcelona, where he witnessed an outbreak of internecine street violence between contending leftist groups. Back at the front, he was shot in the neck by a sniper, the bullet hitting a vocal cord; his doctors assured him he'd never speak again.

Soon after, when the Communists suppressed the Trotskyists on the pretext that they were consorting with the Fascists—a ridiculous charge —Orwell, fearing arrest, fled across the French border and thence to England. In London, he wrote, were "the men in bowler hats, the pigeons in Trafalgar Square, the red buses, the blue policemen—all sleeping the deep, deep sleep of England, from which I sometimes fear that we shall never wake till we are jerked out of it by the roar of bombs."

On his return, with the outcome of the war still in doubt, Orwell wrote about what he'd seen in a plain, forthright style almost wholly free of sentimentalism and cant: *Homage to Catalonia*, one critic has written, is "perhaps the best book that exists on the Spanish Civil War." Wrote another, Lionel Trilling, "This book is one of the important documents of our time."

Though permeated by the mud, lice, boredom, and fatigue of front line combat, *Homage to Catalonia* is no antiwar tract. As horrifying as the war was, Orwell did not regard it as meaningless. He had signed up to help save Spain from Franco. He knew there was plenty of killing to be done. He was not a pacifist. At one point, he writes of a "trainload of fresh men gliding proudly up the line, the maimed men sliding slowly down, and all the while the guns on the open trucks making one's heart leap as guns always do." The sight revived in him, he wrote, "that pernicious feeling, so difficult to get rid of, that war is glorious after all."

Orwell's chronicle is redolent of his fondness for the Spanish people, "with their innate decency and their ever-present Anarchist tinge" (even as he missed good, sturdy English justice). And just a hint of travelogue here overlies the gritty combat narrative.

But what almost compels a reading of Orwell's book today is his incisive account of the infighting that racked the loyalist Left even as it waged war on the Right. Here, Orwell and his time resonate with us and ours. For in dissecting the Communist subjugation of the other loyalist parties, he exposes a recurrent and troubling axiom of modern political life: The more tender and progressive the ideals professed, the more they're apt to cover up cruelty, ruthlessness and lies. It's a theme he further developed in *Animal Farm* and *1984*. It can scarcely bear too much repeating today.

Yet Orwell was himself an idealist. He had "breathed the air of equality," he wrote. "The Spanish militias, while they lasted, were a sort of microcosm of a classless society...where no one was on the make, where there was a shortage of everything but no privilege and no bootlicking...It deeply attracted me."

But above all, Orwell was honest: He showed it was possible to hold passionate convictions—and even be ready to kill or be killed for them —without ever letting them cloud his clear vision or inhibit his telling of what was true. ❖

# Civilization and Its Discontents

### By Sigmund Freud
### First published in 1930

Freud has taken his lumps of late. Sleep lab data may supply a better way to understand dreams, many now suspect, than do his notions of wish-fulfillment and repression. Discoveries in brain chemistry give his theories of neurosis, once revolutionary, a musty, shopworn air.

Still, there were good reasons Freud enjoyed intellectual popularity for so long, and they owe as much to the sheer force of his personality, and the eloquence with which he expressed it in print, as they do to the validity of his theories. We see an example of this in Civilization and Its Discontents, one of Freud's last works, published in 1930.

Men and women stand in continual tension with society, Freud wrote. We may wish to act on our instinctual sex drive unhindered, yet family, society and personal conscience restrain us. We may wish to string up our enemies from the nearest tree, but the force of law and the opinion of our fellows stops us. Civilization cramps our style, and so stirs in us a malaise. We each deal with this conflict differently, adopting one or another strategy for reconciling personal needs with the dictates of society. Invariably, there's a price to pay, often in the form of neurosis.

Therein lies the essence of this slim book. But its rewards lie less in its ideas than in the opportunity it furnishes to brush up against the author's formidable personality. Freud is all force, his words brimming with confidence and authority. There are few appeals to case histories or scientific studies here, no mind-numbing recitation of bibliographic sources.

"What we call happiness," he declares, "comes from the (preferably sudden) satisfaction of needs which have been damned up to a high degree, and it is from its nature only possible as an episodic phenomenon. When any situation that is desired by the pleasure principle is prolonged, it only produces a feeling of mild contentment. We are so made that we can derive intense enjoyment only from a contrast and very little from a state of things."

*We are so made*...as if he were privy to the blueprints!

The whole book is written that way. When Freud does deign to hedge his bets, you notice it—as when he suggests a link between family structure and the weak role of smell, among humans, in sexual excitement: "This," he admits, "is only a theoretical speculation." (Of course, he adds immediately, it's "important enough to deserve careful checking.")

But this hint of humility startles by its rarity. More often, we feel in the presence of an all-wise father, uttering truths culled from infinite human experience, and from the orbit of whose intellect we can scarcely wrest ourselves: "An unrestricted satisfaction of every need presents itself as the most enticing method of conducting one's life," Freud declares, "but it means putting enjoyment before caution, and soon brings its own punishment."

Sometimes, his counsel sounds like that of an Eastern guru: "All suffering is nothing else than sensation; it only exists in so far as we feel it."

Sometimes Freud is prophetic, as when—almost half a century before the discovery of enkephalins in the brain—he posits "substances in the chemistry of our own bodies" that can leave us intoxicated.

Herr Freud on technology: "This newly won power over space and time, this subjugation of the forces of nature, which is the fulfillment of a longing that goes back thousands of years, has not increased the amount of pleasurable satisfaction which [we] may expect from life and has not made [us] feel happier."

Civilization, says Freud, is the arena for the great "struggle between Eros and Death," between the constructive and destructive forces forever at war within the human species. "And it is this battle of the giants," he says, in a swipe at traditional religion, "that our nurse-maids try to appease with their lullaby about Heaven." ❖

# *Arrowsmith*

*By Sinclair Lewis*
*First published in 1925*

Subtle it ain't.

The characters in *Arrowsmith*, Sinclair Lewis' novel about medical research, are, well, *characters*. Almus Pickerbaugh is the fervent public health director out to cheerlead and cow his street-spitting fellow citizens to the One True Way of Health. Max Gottlieb is the ascetic researcher devoted to Truth. Gustaf Sondelius is the boisterous, big-hearted, hard-drinking Swedish field scientist who can charm rats into turning over dead in their plague-bearing tracks. So faithfully do Lewis' characters run true to type that when one of them does not—for instance, the officious research director Rippletown Holabird (love those names?)—you want to cheer.

No, don't read *Arrowsmith* for nuances of personality.

And don't read it for the plot, the twists and turns of which are often telegraphed in advance and are not entirely believable at that. As when the book's idealistic protagonist, Martin Arrowsmith, by now a scientist of international standing, treks off to the Vermont woods to set up his test tubes untrammeled by bureaucratic overseers, discarding rich wife and child along the way.

Nor will the reader encounter great profundity here. Nor depths of poignancy. Nor sublime revelations.

No, one reads Lewis in general, and *Arrowsmith* in particular, for the chance to view the world through a rare, finely polished lens that shows up, in sometimes painful relief, the frailties of human nature and the superficialities of social intercourse.

Born in the tiny red brick town of Elk Mills in the fictional Midwestern state of Winnemac, Martin Arrowsmith wants to be a doctor.

# Roughing It

*By Mark Twain*
*First published in 1873*

*Roughing It* is grand fun.

There's Mark Twain, age twenty-six, starting a campfire. There's Mark Twain, failing to mind it. There's a whole pine forest in the Nevada Territory going up in flames.

Another time the distractible Twain releases the bridles of the horses—who wander off, leaving him and his friends without food or water in the middle of a blizzard.

Lapses like these may well account for Twain's checkered employment history, as riverboat pilot, grocery clerk, law student, blacksmith, printer. He was, apparently, wholly unsuited to any of life's work—any, that is, but expressing the soul of Middle America in the nineteenth century.

*Roughing It* is travelogue, autobiography, history and compendium of Wild West lore all in one: The author, accompanying his brother to Nevada in the summer of 1861, stays six years. Beginning with the three-week overland stage crossing from St. Joseph, Missouri, *Roughing It* is the hearty, always entertaining chronicle of his adventures. In the full exuberance of youth, Twain already commands considerable literary powers.

Many of the stock characters of Hollywood Western lore make early appearances in these pages: Slade, the ultimate desperado—a cold-blooded killer of twenty-six men, who ultimately dies on the gallows at the hands of vigilantes grown weary of his excesses of frontier bullyism; Slade's wife, "a brave, loving, spirited woman," who rides to the rescue, but too late.

And the Pony Express rider who gallops on alone, astride a "little wafer of a racing saddle," with letters at five dollars' postage each strapped under his thighs—250 miles a day across the prairies and deserts. As Twain and the others aboard the overland stage spot him in the distance, "every neck is stretched further, and every eye strained wider. Away across the endless dead level of the prairie a black speck appears against the sky, and it is plain that it moves."

Much of the author's abundant fancy mixes with facts here. And yet with every tall tale, every flight of hyperbole, the reader encounters a tell-tale clue to set the record straight. Twain gives a man's name as "Brown," but is quick to inform us that "any name would do." He tells us that a toothless old woman first reported as 165 years old may not be: "Being in calmer mood, now, I voluntarily knock off 100 years." Despite humor and snap, Twain is no journalistic airhead. Wild yarns interspersed with soberly objective reportage yield few doubts as to which is which.

That's important: Because as entertaining as all this is, the book's seventy-nine little chapters also come down to us as a potentially invaluable resource on Americana. For instance, wearied of hearing the same Horace Greeley story half a dozen times, Twain pleads with yet another prospective teller to "rather tell me about young George Washington and his little hatchet for a change"—suggesting how legendary *that* story had already become.

And has any historian ever given us a better-drawn portrait of the American boom town than Twain's of Virginia City and the other towns of the Comstock Lode? Has any naturalist better briefly captured the beauty of a still-virgin Lake Tahoe? Has any linguist offered a funnier celebration of Western slang than the scene in which "Scotty" Briggs makes funeral arrangements with the new pastor just in from back East?

Twain explores terrain almost wholly male: To read it, one would think these lusty boom towns had no dance-hall girls, no wives, no mothers—no women in any capacity whatever—and that neither sex nor

# A Study in Scarlet

*By Sir Arthur Conan Doyle*
*First published in 1887*

He never lived, say the miserly in spirit. Yet now, with the Victorian London in which he never lived a hundred years gone, he lives.

A brand of English spring water immortalizes the address, 221b Baker Street, at which he never lived. A remark he never uttered introduces a chapter about memory in an American psychology text. The Late Movie dramatizes exploits he never performed.

Sherlock Holmes, the turn-of-the-century English detective, was the creation of one physician's imagination. Yet Holmes has gained so devoted a following, has become so much part of our cultural vocabulary, that it seems to us as if he did live. (In *The People's Almanac*, in fact, a biography of him appears, along with those of such other historical figures as Superman, Tarzan and the Lone Ranger.)

It is in *A Study in Scarlet*, first in a series of four novels and fifty-six short stories, that Sir Arthur Conan Doyle breathed life into Holmes, and in it many of the elements of the Holmesian legend can already be seen: The hansom cabs clattering along cobblestoned London streets. Holmes's blustering counterparts at Scotland Yard, Gregson and Lestrade. The landlady forever admitting to his quarters in Baker Street the makings of some new twist of plot.

And above all, Holmes himself. The miracle is that even after all the Basil Rathbones have played him in film and on the air, after countless successors to Conan Doyle have milked him for one new story after another, after a thousand magnifying glasses and ten thousand deerstalker caps have passed before our eyes as the veritable signature of the sleuthing profession, Holmes remains as fresh as ever. That he's not stale with age and overexposure by now testifies to the sheer magic of the Conan Doyle creation—a magic that rests not on such trappings as deer-stalker cap and inverness cape but on Holmes' very character.

"I have found it! I have found it!" exults Holmes over a laboratory discovery he's just made as Dr. Watson is introduced to him for the first time. "Had he discovered a gold mine, greater delight could not have shown upon his features," remarks Watson. Surely this boyish enthusiasm, this single-minded concentration on the matter at hand, this unselfconscious joy at simply doing what he's doing, is part of what makes Holmes unforgettable.

Ah, but let us not forget the story in this short novel; there *is* a story, and rather a good one, in this, Holmes' and Watson's first case together: An American from Cleveland is found dead in a vacant suburban house, with the inscription RACHE written in blood on the wall above the corpse. At the end of Part I, Holmes himself apprehends the murderer in a scene that looks as if it were written for the movies, though it preceded the first commercial motion picture by almost a decade. Part II transports the reader into the American Far West for the origins of the crime, and in the final pages Holmes tells how he deduced the identity of the culprit.

Sometimes, I am bound to report, it all seems a little far-fetched. The basis of the Holmes method is that the smallest clues may reveal important truths, and that one need only proceed through a series of logically connected steps to arrive at a solution. But does the mere appearance of a wedding band at the scene of the crime imply, as Holmes insists it does, that "Clearly the murderer had used it to remind his victim of some dead or absent woman?" Does the appearance of blood, when signs of struggle are not otherwise evident, give reason to think the perpetrator of the crime had sprung a nosebleed in his excitement and so is "a robust and ruddy-faced man?"

No matter. It is not to cavil at holes in his logic that we read the adventures of Sherlock Holmes. It is to stand in the presence of a uniquely engaging character who enjoys himself and his work. ❖

# The Song of Hiawatha

*By Henry Wadsworth Longfellow*
*First published in 1855*

Poets, "serious" ones at least, no longer write like Henry Wadsworth Longfellow, no longer write epic poems like *The Song of Hiawatha.*

*Hiawatha* is frankly sentimental. It calls up a part of our national story—American Indian life before the white man—that many of us would as soon leave to the two paragraphs our textbooks ordinarily give it. It lacks every trace of the hard-edged cynicism of our age. Its hero is a hero, not an anti-hero, spy or gangster. And it's written in a verse form that cries to be read *out loud.*

But *Hiawatha* can be wonderful—if you, in turn, can suspend your end-of-the-century skepticism and confront, like a child again, the occasional nobility of our species; if you're willing to meet a moccasin-clad primitive who talks to birds and prays to the Great Spirit; who tenderly cares for his wife, named Laughing Water; who devotedly loves his brothers-in-spirit, Kwasind and Chibiabos; who seeks only good for his people, the Ojibways, and peace for all the Indian Nation.

Longfellow was "overpraised in his time, underrated in our own," as one critic sums up his reputation as a poet. But this product of an old-line New England family, who went to school with Franklin Pierce and Nathaniel Hawthorne, was a scholar, too. He taught at Bowdoin College and at Harvard. He was a world traveler, an expert linguist. His Maine boyhood, when local tribes still inhabited surrounding forests, inspired his interest in American Indian culture—though he at first knew little about the history, arts, superstitions, customs or religions in which *The Song of Hiawatha* is so steeped.

A Mohawk chief named Hiawatha did, as it happens, once live;

history credits him with bringing warring Iroquois tribes together in peace. But there all likeness between fact and fiction ends. Longfellow's study of the *Kalevala*, a Finnish epic, furnished him with the rhythm, and some of the story, of his own epic. And the writings of Henry Rowe Schoolcraft, who for thirteen years lived with Great Lakes Indian tribes, at last gave him the locale, the lore and the legends he could weave into *Hiawatha.*

And oh, what lovely legends they are: How the four winds came to be, and how Mudjekeewis, the West Wind, seduced the daughter of Nokomis, who "bore a son of love and sorrow/Thus was born my Hiawatha." How Hiawatha thrice wrestled Mondamin, overcame him and buried him as he had asked to be buried: "Make a bed for me to lie in/Where the rain may fall upon me/Where the sun may come and warm me"—and from whose grave grew man's first corn.

This is a *song* of Hiawatha, and it draws much of its impact from its music—from the relentless, hypnotic cadence of its unrhymed trochaic tetrameter ("BY the SHORES OF GITCH-e GU-me, BY the SHIN-ing BIG sea WA-ter"); from its insistent alliteration; from its uncannily powerful repetition; from its sense-dripping naturalistic imagery...

There comes a time in reading *Hiawatha* not unlike what one experiences on a camping vacation, about the fourth day out: the abrupt realization that all those meadows, brooks and woods, all those deer and squirrels, herons and gulls, are not just another "attraction" somehow in competition with the city, but things apart, in a world of their own, something unspoiled by humans that must remain so. Longfellow's epic sounds just such a profoundly reverential note.

It's easy to make fun of all this. *Hiawatha* is like a poem rated "G," for General Audiences, that "sophisticated" readers may too readily disdain. It does speak of battles and blood, of famine and toil; yet it never submerges the reader in it, keeps him ever at a safe distance. Its terrain is tender sentiments—which, sadly, often leaves *Hiawatha* consigned to the children's room at the library. As if the rest of us, adults, have nothing to learn from Hiawatha's goodness. As if we have no business being inspired by the nobility of Hiawatha's character. ❖

ROBERT   KANIGEL

# The Rise of David Levinsky

*By Abraham Cahan*
*First published in 1917*

"For my first meal in the New World I bought a three-cent wedge of
coarse rye bread, off a huge round loaf, on a stand on Essex Street."

Our immigrant forebears, any we know yet alive, mostly come to us
as wrinkled, creaking octogenarians. How breathtaking, then, to be
plunked down into their own time, to meet them as youths newly come to
these shores!

*The Rise of David Levinsky* has been called an "unrivaled record of
a great historical experience." Through it, the Lower East Side that the
immigrant Jews filled to bursting with their numbers and their energy
reaches us as they themselves experienced it—their youthful faces
turned in hope, and some anxiety, toward their American future.

All the cliches of the immigrant experience come alive: David
Levinsky arrives in New York, at the receiving center known as Castle
Garden, fresh from a little town in Russia, and is immediately swept up
into the city's streets. His head is full of Talmud, that many-volumed body
of rabbinic commentary that speaks of the relationship of man to man and
of man to God. His heart is with his dead mother, killed by town rowdies
back in Russia. He must find a place to sleep. He must find means of
livelihood.

Whatever he was, he can no longer be; America is too different.
"The scurry and bustle of the people were not merely overwhelmingly
greater...than in my native town. It was of another sort. The swing and
step of the pedestrians, the voices and manner of the street peddlers, and
a hundred and one other things seemed to testify to far more self-confi-
dence and energy, to larger ambitions and wider scopes."

153

So America takes this pious Talmud student and makes of him a millionaire manufacturer of women's dresses. *The Rise of David Levinsky* chronicles just how—and tells of the price he paid in loneliness, severed roots and diminished spirit.

This is a story of our grandparents and great-grandparents, of what America did to them and what they did to it; it is a story of our middle past, that magically compelling interlude of years every generation possesses...The distant past, of Crusades and Renaissance, comes to us straight from the history books, and so may forever remain remote. The recent past—the times we ourselves remember, like the moon landing or the O.J. Simpson trial—suffer from overfamiliarity. It's the middle past— that time just beyond our own that we read about in books and also hear about from those who have lived it—that is most apt to be left awash in feeling. Such a time may cast a bewitching spell, but also become prey to sentiment and nostalgic distortion.

This is what *David Levinsky*—"a minor masterpiece of genre realism," Irving Howe has called it—so adroitly sidesteps. Written by journalist Abraham Cahan, who for half a century edited what was arguably the premier Yiddish newspaper in the world, the *Jewish Daily Forward*, it works by piling up journalistic detail—even if the piling is done with little stylistic grace.

No one pines away for abstractions like "the Old Country" here. Rather, Levinsky longingly recalls the "huddle of ramshackle one-story houses" known as Abner's Court in which he lived with his mother. The crowded streets of the Lower East Side live in Levinsky's memory concretely, in the image of "a big, florid-faced huckster shouting at the top of his husky voice: 'Strawberri-i-ies, strawberri-i-ies, five cents a quart!' "

There's much more to *Levinsky*, of course, than this. Like the poignant story of a failed romantic life standing beside magnificent business success. And the implied indictment, in Levinsky's ultimate loneliness, of a soulless America. Finally, in the way the book recalls how

Jewish immigrants, almost by themselves, built the modern ladies' garment industry, it stands, as John Higham once wrote in the introduction to a 1960 edition, "among the best novels of American business."

Mr. Higham noted that since its publication, "this memorable novel has received more respect than attention." *Levinsky* is memorable and deserves the respect—but also, for anyone wishing to understand the American Jew at century's end, the attention. ❖

# *Java Head*

*By Joseph Hergesheimer*
*First published in 1918*

*Java Head* is set in the New England port of Salem in the mid-nine-teenth century. It is a time when swift new clipper ships are transforming the shipping business, when smaller, less commercially aggressive towns like Salem are being left behind by Boston and New York. The whole story takes place here, on land, yet is tinged with the romance of the sea and the mystery of the Orient.

The Ammidons are a prosperous shipping family who live in a home that the crusty old patriarch of the clan, Jeremy, has built and named "Java Head," with its intimations of safe harbor reached after a storm-tossed voyage. His son William lives there with his wife Rhoda and their four daughters, and runs the family business, through he's scarcely set foot on a sailing vessel. Jeremy's other son, Gerrit, is a ship's captain with little interest in the business side of shipping, and little use for the weary conventions of the land. As the book opens, he and his ship, *Nautilus*, are months late in returning to port.

Then Gerrit does come home, which is when the trouble begins. For he brings with him a wife. Her name is Taou Yuen, and she is a Manchu princess.

The family, the whole town, are flabbergasted. If America already trumpeted its pluralism back then, Salem did not. And Taou Yuen, in her white powdered face and flowery silks, with her emotional reserve and heathen ways, is enough to leave the locals speechless. No one can believe Gerrit has actually married her. Indeed—and this forms a central premise of the story—most don't consider their union legitimate at all. "What I can't understand," says brother William, "is why you call it a marriage, why you brought your woman here to us, to Rhoda and the children."

One townsperson, however, reacts otherwise. Edward Dunsack, son of an old shipmate of Jeremy, has spent years in China and become infected with its mysteries. Edward speaks Chinese fluently, sees himself as far above Salem's crude occidental sensibilities, fancies himself more spiritually congenial with the Manchu noblewoman—and sets out to steal her from her husband.

To do that, he turns to Nettie Vollar, the illegitimate daughter of his sister and the visible object of Gerrit's attentions last time he was home. Their relationship broken up by Edward's Bible-thumping father, Nettie has been left emotionally crippled. Now Edward plots to enlist her, and her anguish, in his efforts to gain Taou Yuen for himself.

The anchor to the story—solid, constant, immutable—is Salem and its denizens. Yet only William, among the main characters, truly fits in— and he's portrayed as lackluster and self-righteous. Virtually all the other major characters cling to the fringes of town life. Gerrit is more at home on a heaving quarterdeck than amid the "nauseous hypocrisy, the pretension of a piety covering commercial dishonesty, obscenity of thought and spreading scandal" of Salem, and seems ineffably drawn to those the town rejects. Such as Tauo Yuen, heathen and foreigner. Or the notorious Nettie, largely excluded from Salem's social life. Edward, meanwhile, safe in his darkened room, smokes opium and dresses in black silk Chinese robes.

*Java Head*, then, is about individuals at war with their time and their surroundings. The house of that name embodies the tension— between all that's safe and familiar on Pleasant Street, and the dark appeal of foreign places and foreign ways.

Hergesheimer's story employs two special vocabularies—that of the sea and of the Orient. But while he's plainly studied up on them, he consigns them to ghettos within the book. We witness Taou Yuen's elaborate make-up rituals; Dunsack's reveries on Chinese wisdom; Jeremy's salty sea monologues. But they feel alien, incompletely integrated into the book. This intriguing novel retains the stamp of Salem far more than it does that of the Orient, or of the sea.

In a myriad of ways it says, *You are the place and the circumstances out of which you came, and never any other.* ❖

# Mr. Pottermack's Oversight

*By R. Austin Freeman*
*First published in 1930*

Why do so many otherwise gripping murder mysteries keep you in suspense for three hundred pages and then, in the final paragraphs, leave you feeling cheated?

R. Austin Freeman's *Mr. Pottermack's Oversight* proves it needn't be. Here's a mystery with the ultimate in satisfying endings. The reader's faith is rewarded, his questions answered. Everybody gets what he or she deserves. Love conquers.

Of course, considering that the murder occurs at the outset, and that we know who did it, and why, this is one murder mystery that's no mystery at all: A loathsome, lumbering bear of a man, James Lewson, calls at the quiet country home of Marcus Pottermack, a clean-featured gentleman of lively intelligence. Blackmail is Lewson's game; Pottermack's past can stand no scrutiny. But Lewson has come calling one time too many. Pottermack won't pay. Lewson rages. The men fight. Pottermack knocks him against the stone edge of the garden well, killing him. Lewson's body slides down the well. "From the black pit issued vague, echoing murmurs, followed presently by a hollow, reverberating splash; and after that, silence."

Chapter two, of eighteen, is not yet over.

The next day, it's discovered that a clerk named Lewson has absconded with bank funds; no one suspects him dead. Dr. John Thorndyke, a medically-trained detective, takes an unofficial interest in the case. Soon, he's poking around Pottermack's gate (and spying on him over the garden wall with a periscope camouflaged as a cane). The book is barely a third through and Thorndyke's hot on the scent. The plot is unraveling entirely too quickly, it seems, to sustain for long.

Not to worry: ahead is Pottermack's impossible dilemma, furtive midnight treks into the woods, a coroner's inquest, and the final confrontation between the protagonists. Along the way, we meet some of England's finest pickpockets—and one of Egypt's most revolting mummies.

Traditional roles blur here. The detective is, as usual, relentless and shrewd, if a little too dryly cerebral. It's the killer who's the sympathetic character—admirable save only for having killed a man and tried to get away with it. And besides, he loves the widow Mrs. Bellard; his love is pure and—secret revealed!—goes back years. Indeed, the novel's suspense lies not alone in whether the killer will be caught, nor in how the sleuth will catch him, but in Pottermack's precise fate—which comes to matter more to us than that justice be served or that Thorndyke get his man.

Throughout, our travels with author Freeman through England's quiet country lanes are a delight. His language has an old fashioned charm not seen much since Ernest Hemingway changed how people wrote. Nor is he shy about occasionally intruding into the story, being perfectly capable of observing, say, that "Readers who have followed this history to its present stage will have realized by this time that Mr. Pottermack was a gentleman of uncommon tenacity of purpose."

And yet the story itself moves by no means as leisurely as the sentences that tell it; it's an easy read, quick as well as satisfying, honeyed with little surprises. Pottermack, for instance, turns out to have a more checkered history than his easy workshop puttering and country gentleman's leisure might suggest. It's not giving away too much of the plot to reveal that he's not always lived in his lovely English cottage. Or that his name is a made-up one—drawn, as it happens, from an American river.

It was in the *Columbo* TV series of some years back that the inverted detective story—where the murderer is revealed from the beginning—reached new heights. *Mr. Pottermack's Oversight*, written half a century before, could have been its inspiration. ❖

# A Bell for Adano

By John Hersey
First published in 1944

This is no garden variety war propaganda.

Appearing at a time when Allied armies battled the Nazis for Europe, and drenched in a nectar of democracy, decency, and respect for the Common Man, *A Bell for Adano* might be written off—rashly, it turns out—as mere propaganda. It takes little imagination to picture twenty-nine-year-old *Time* correspondent John Hersey being importuned by the War Department to work up a yarn for the home front on the evils of fascism and the glories of American democracy. Indeed, a previous book by Hersey had been cited as recommended reading by the Council on Books in Wartime, and *A Bell for Adano* itself became a book club pick and a best seller. Plainly, it told Americans what they wanted to hear about their country and why they were fighting, and served the nation's wartime interests.

The novel is set in Sicily in the wake of the Allied invasion; the Americans have come and Mussolini's town officials have run for the surrounding hills. Our hero is Maj. Victor Joppolo, the town's civil affairs officer, who sets up shop in the town hall, the office of the deposed fascist mayor, Signor Nasta. To see Nasta, townspeople had had to make appointments weeks ahead. With the American major, they just drop by and speak their minds.

Soon they realize they can get justice from the man they call Mister Major, that he has their interests at heart, and can deliver what they need. That includes food, clean streets, fairness, and a replacement for their golden-toned, seven-hundred-year-old church bell, carted off by Mussolini's men to make cannon. Joppolo sets about getting one. Later, an American general, in a fit of pique at being delayed by a slow-witted Italian peasant and his mule, orders all mules out of town; Joppolo quietly countermands the order—a transgression which, despite snafus enough to resurrect every stereotype of American bureaucratic laxity, ultimately catches up with him.

All through the novel, Hersey contrasts injustices suffered under the fascist yoke with the fairness and decency of the Americans. Joppolo is serious about instilling in them American ideals. "Perhaps you do not know what a democracy is," he tells town officials gathered around him. "I will tell you..." And in a speech sure to bring chills to every civics teacher, he does.

Still, if this be propaganda, it's propaganda with a twist. For one thing, Joppolo, this representative of all that's solid and square about America, is no heartland small towner but a mustachioed first-generation Italian-American from the Bronx. And the villain of the piece is not one of Mussolini's strutting minions but another American—an American general, no less.

What species of propaganda is this that depicts an American general with the brutish insensitivity of a Nazi storm trooper? Or that shows American GIs routinely failing to carry out their orders? Or lusting after the local girls instead of keeping their minds on wives and sweethearts back home? Or, quartered in Italian homes, drunkenly destroying works of antiquity left in their care? This is supposed to buoy up morale and rev up the folks back home?

So then again, maybe *A Bell for Adano* is not propaganda, or at least not only propaganda.

Or else, maybe half a century ago the gap between "propaganda" and how Americans saw themselves as a nation was not so wide as it is today. Maybe Americans back then had not yet grown distrustful of noble sentiments. Maybe, during what Studs Terkel has called "The Good War," it was plainer than it sometimes is now that real differences existed between political and social systems, that those differences mattered, and that, compared to others, our system was a good one.

Sadly, the cynicism with which many readers are apt to greet Hersey's story tells us more about today's American than we may wish to know. ❖

# The Martian Chronicles

*By Ray Bradbury*
*First published in 1950*

Martians inhabit Ray Bradbury's Mars, but they're apt to spark scant interest among readers of *The Martian Chronicles*. For in this classic, from the same flowering of post-World War II science fiction talent that produced the likes of Asimov, Heinlein and Clarke, Bradbury's focus never veers far from that noisy, violent, infuriating intragalactic species known as man.

*The Martian Chronicles* is a novel—actually a series of connected short stories—that recounts the exploration and colonization of the fourth planet by successive waves of earthlings. It is set in the concluding months of the twentieth century and the early twenty-first.

The earliest explorers are treated by the Martians as ripe for the madhouse; even the continued existence of their spaceship after the impatient Martian psychologist Mr. Xxx has zapped them into nothingness fails to convince him they were ever anything but their own hallucinations. Later, a sixteen-man expedition is seemingly greeted by a whole town of loving friends and family, welcomed into their vintage 1926 homes—complete with bead curtains and Maxfield Parrish paintings—and then are quietly destroyed in the night by their mischievous Martian hosts.

Finally, though, colonization efforts succeed, and men and women begin settling Mars just as earlier pioneers settled the old American west, displaying all the greed and plundering instincts of their predecessors. "They were leaving bad wives or bad jobs or bad towns." Bradbury writes of them. "They were coming to find something or leave something or get something, to dig up something or bury something or leave something alone. They were coming with small dreams or large dreams or none at all. But a government finger pointed from four-color posters in many towns. 'There's Work for You in the Sky: See Mars!' and the men shuffled forward."

In the year 2003, the settlers "brought in 15,000 lumber feet of Oregon pine to build Tenth City...and they hammered together a clean, neat little town by the edge of the stone canals...It was as if...a great earthquake had shaken loose the roots and cellars of an Iowa town, and then, in an instant, a whirlwind twister of Oz-like proportions had carried the entire town off to Mars to set it down without a bump..."

This, in fact, is just how Bradbury handles bigotry and book burning, environmental desecration and war: He has transplanted it all to Mars and "set it down without a bump." The new Martians build towns, operate hot-dog stands, experience the loneliness of the frontier, bicker among themselves and bristle at the encroachments of the Feds back on Earth. They inhabit Mars, yet remain earthlings.

What raises all this above the Midwestern flatness in which Bradbury was raised, and for which he plainly feels a nostalgic tug, is the poetry of his prose. "Full grown without memory, the robots waited. In green silks the color of forest pools, in silks the color of frog and fern, they waited." Or, "The girl, in the gunfire, in the heat, in the concussion, folded like a soft scarf, melted like a crystal figurine. What was left of her, ice, snowflake, smoke, blew away in the wind." *The Martian Chronicles* are full of such stuff—lyrical, dreamlike, ethereal.

Just as they're full of a chill, cackling terror that pops up at the oddest moments. As when Capt. John Black guesses that his older brother, whom he thought long dead, is actually a Martian-conceived figment of his dreams. He slips away from the bed they share. "Where do you think you're going?" his brother says, his voice now "quite cold."

Or as when Walter Gripp, the last man left on an abruptly depopulated planet, finally meets the last woman, Genevieve: "Her face...was round and thick, and her eyes were like two immense eggs stuck into a white mess of bread dough. Her legs were as big around as the stumps of trees, and she moved with an ungainly shuffle...She had no lips at all."

No, Martian setting or not, this is not really science fiction. Indeed, grubby scientified details about the hostile Martian atmosphere or rocket payload seem to worry Bradbury not a bit. They would worry the reader equally little except that curiosity about them occasionally threatens to waylay interest in the story itself. On the other hand, the stories don't risk growing outdated with every new cyber-marvel or NASA space extravaganza.

But something else does date them. Though set at the turn of the twenty-first century, Bradbury's stories reek of the postwar period in which they were written: The cult of prosperity...the early stirrings of black discontent...the intolerant stupidity of the McCarthy years...the recurrent nostalgia for an America that depression and war had destroyed. All these ride Bradbury's rockets to Mars, weighing them down with cultural baggage. After all, the Deep South general storekeeper incensed at the uppitiness of sharecropper blacks is not so familiar a character anymore, and his ranks diminish with each passing day. Dated characters like him detract from these stories in a way wholly imagined ones—green-eyed, antenna-sprouting Venusians, say—never would.

*The Martian Chronicles* suffer the way a ten-year-old automobile does: Too old to gleam with its original sparkle, too new to qualify as antique. A few years more will age them to perfection. ❖

ROBERT KANIGEL

# Gentleman's Agreement

*By Laura Z. Hobson*
*First appeared in 1947*

A writer gets a magazine assignment for a series of articles on anti-Semitism. His first reaction: How can he make the subject interesting and relevant to his readers? How can he avoid the customary recitation of wrongs, the preaching, the moral smugness, that the subject so readily provokes?

For sixty-three pages of *Gentleman's Agreement*, the writer agonizes, trying and rejecting one approach after another. (For this glimpse into the creative process alone, the novel deserves a reading.) Finally, one evening as he's pacing his room, the solution sneaks up on him: He'll be a Jew. "Six weeks, eight weeks, nine months—however long it takes. Christ, I've got it."

The writer is new to New York, the novel's setting; he knows hardly a soul. His name, Phil Green, marks him as neither indelibly Jewish nor not. And so, with the blessing of his editor, he sets out upon his journalistic adventure.

When Phil remarks that he's made an appointment to see a Jewish doctor, his mother's physician lifts an eyebrow, then concedes that Dr. Abrahams is "not given to overcharging and running visits out, the way some do..."

A journalist friend starts to ask Phil whether or not he'd been for Franklin D. Roosevelt, then interrupts himself: "Sure, you would be..."

Little things: "That's all these first days had given him," Phil thinks. "No yellow armband, no marked park bench, no Gestapo...But day by day the little thump of insult. Day by day the tapping on the nerves, the delicate assault on the proud stuff of a man's identity..."

# The Ten Books of Architecture

*By Vitruvius*
*Written circa 25 B.C.*

Sand mixed with mortar to form cement should be mostly free of dirt. To check, sprinkle some on a white garment, then shake it off. If the garment stays clean, the sand is suitable.

So advised Marcus Vitruvius Pollio, the first century B.C. Roman architect and military engineer whose *Ten Books of Architecture* powerfully influenced the Renaissance. Generations of architects followed his prescriptions, sometimes slavishly—in part because of his practical knowledge, in part his authoritative tone, in part his sheer comprehensiveness.

"I have observed, Emperor," writes Vitruvius in his introduction to Book IV, addressing Augustus, "that many in their treatises and volumes of commentaries on architecture have not presented the subject with well-ordered completeness." This shortcoming he meant to correct.

Vitruvius offers a primer in the architecture of temples, theaters, public forums, baths, private houses. He discusses principles of harmony and proportion. He ranges over terrain as varied as the layout of rooms in private homes, the design of siege weapons, the building of retaining walls, and means of finding underground springs.

An architect, says Vitruvius, should know enough about music to properly tune the bronze vessels then used in theaters to resonate with an actor's voice. He should know enough history, for example, to explain that caryatids—sculpted female figures in flowing robes that serve as columns in some Greek buildings—originally marked the punishment of the Peloponnesian state of Caryae for siding with the Persians, the sculptures commemorating the slavery of its women.

Vitruvius' ten books do not merely set out general principles; they are full of numerical proportions, specific advice, injunctions. In a temple whose arrangement of columns follows the diastyle pattern, the space between columns, we learn, must be three columns wide. To make a blue pigment, grind together flowers of natron with sand, then mix in coarsely grated bits of copper, roll the mixture into balls and place them in an oven. "As soon as the copper and the sand grow hot and unite under the intensity of the fire, they mutually receive each other's sweat...[and] are reduced to a blue color."

Vitruvius advises that the architrave, which rests upon the columns, should be disproportionately larger than the longer columns supporting it—one-twelfth the column height for columns of twenty-five to thirty feet, but only a thirteenth for columns fifteen to twenty feet long. "For the higher that the eye has to climb, the less easily can it make its way through the thicker and thicker mass of air."

Such would-be scientific explanations might reasonably undermine our confidence in the architectural precepts of Marcus Vitruvius Pollio. Still, Renaissance architects like Alberti and Bramante, Michelangelo and Palladio, drew inspiration from him, and followed his advice. And they hardly disgraced themselves.

Architects in quest of ancient wisdom, however, should not be the only ones to read Vitruvius. "The men of old were born like the wild beasts, in woods, caves and droves, and lived on savage fare," he begins a chapter on the origin of houses. And while his architectural knowledge was the product of eons of civilization, he was still two thousand years closer to "men of old" than we are now. Reading him, then, takes us back to a time when the built world was not so taken for granted; when a brick was not a standardized thirty-cent building material, defined by long-established engineering specifications.

Clean water must be found, strong walls erected. Sand, lime, flooring, stucco? Their use in building, we're reminded here, is a product of civilization, of men and women trying and failing and trying again, of teaching themselves and passing their hard-won knowledge to later generations.

Within this dry architectural treatise lurks a surprisingly inspiring tale of our species.

ROBERT KANIGEL

# The Lives of the Most Eminent Italian Architects, Painters, and Sculptors

*By Giorgio Vasari*
*First published in 1550, revised and enlarged in 1568*

Giorgio Vasari was a child of the Renaissance. When he was born in 1511 near Florence, Leonardo da Vinci, Raphael, Titian, and Michelangelo were among the day's working artists. Vasari himself became an architect and painter of no mean note, but by history's more demanding gauge, his were only modest gifts. Today he is best remembered not for his images, which include frescoes in the Palazzo Vecchio, but for his words.

"Without any doubt this figure has put in the shade every other statue, ancient or modern, Greek or Roman...The grace of this figure and the serenity of its pose have never been surpassed, nor have the feet, the hands and the head, whose harmonious proportions and loveliness are in keeping with the rest...Anyone who has seen [it] has no need to see anything else by any other sculptor, living or dead." That's Vasari on Michelangelo's *David,* his judgment reasonable enough, his enthusiasm properly contagious.

Still, by the narrowest literary standards, *The Lives of the Most Eminent Italian Architects, Painters, and Sculptors*—which spans the two centuries from Cimabue and Giotto, through Donatello and Alberti, to Correggio and Michelangelo—exerts only a weak claim on immortality. The biographies follow a none-too-varied format—birth, apprenticeship and early success, leading works, death. They are littered with superlatives that come too freely to be completely trusted. And even making allowance for the vagaries of translation, their prose is uninspired.

While Ruskin's prose is sometimes overwrought, his perceptions are often exquisitely keen, plainly the product of much close viewing throughout the architectural capitals of Europe. Out of the sodden mass of diffuse feeling that overwhelms most of us when confronted with some impressive structure, Ruskin extracts real meaning. Most of us, for example, feel heightened pleasure in the special pleasure in things wrought beautifully by hand; Ruskin conceives in this an offering on the part of the craftsman, a communion between spirits impossible with machine-made products.

A moralistic flavor runs through all this, not surprising in one whose parents were both strict evangelists and who made him, as a child, commit lengthy Bible passages to memory. Sometimes, in a rising crescendo of pulpit oratory, groaning with grand sentiments and dripping with moral fervor, Ruskin lets things get out of hand: "Exactly as a woman of feeling would not wear false jewels, so would a builder of honor disdain false ornaments," he says, mildly enough. But then: "You use that which pretends to have cost, and to be, what it did not, and is not; it is an imposition, a vulgarity, an impertinence, and a sin. Down with it to the ground, grind it to powder, leave its ragged place upon the wall."

All this was written before 1849, when Ruskin was barely thirty. Might he have written otherwise had he been older, more mature, perhaps more balanced in his judgments? We know the answer because a new edition of the book appeared in 1880, with Ruskin's comments on the original sprinkled liberally throughout. It's entertaining to hear the elder Ruskin take the younger to task. But he's no less dogmatic than before, and maybe more.

Back in 1849, for example, Ruskin had condemned heraldic designs as "so professedly and pointedly unnatural that it would be difficult to invent anything uglier." Three decades later, he recants: "This paragraph is wholly false," he writes, without really explaining why, except to say: "Enough is said in praise of heraldry in my later books to atone for this piece of nonsense."

There's other nonsense in *The Seven Lamps of Architecture* for which Ruskin never atones—notions that a century later seem silly or simply arbitrary. For example, while stating categorically that "whatever is pretended is wrong," he argues that ornamental gilding is all right because people are used to the deception by now.

Still, much else here penetrates to the heart of how we see and respond to architecture. After reading it—especially in any edition graced, like the original, with Ruskin's own fine engravings—one is apt never to see a Gothic cathedral in quite the same way again. And even when Ruskin spouts nonsense, his special blustery brand of it is so entertaining it hardly matters. ❖

# The Nude: A Study in Ideal Form

*By Kenneth Clark*
*First published in 1956*

"What is the nude?" asks Kenneth Clark. "It is an art form invented by the Greeks in the fifth century (B.C.), just as opera is an art form invented in seventeenth-century Italy. The conclusion is certainly too abrupt, but it has the merit of emphasizing that the nude is not the subject of art, but a form of art."

Let us be plain: Clark's study of the nude in art is a work of formal scholarship and criticism. Available in book form only through a university publisher, it was originally presented as a lecture series at the National Gallery of Art in 1953. The author writes in a rich Latinate prose that, while elegant, is not easy. His erudition is daunting; many of his references to artists, paintings, and periods will escape the lay reader. And the shades of feeling, the nuances of idea, that he can discern in a work of art are sometimes so gossamer-thin one can scarcely get a hand on them at all.

And yet, of its kind, *The Nude* has already become something of a classic, a work so vigorous and human that it transcends the usual limitations of its form.

Right from the beginning, Clark distinguishes—or rather, as he says in a rhythm characteristic of his prose, "The English language, with its elaborate generosity, distinguishes"—between the naked and the nude. "To be naked is to be deprived of our clothes, and the word implies some of the embarrassment most of us feel in that condition. The word 'nude,' on the other hand, carries, in educated usage, no uncomfortable overtone. The vague image it projects into the mind is not of a huddled and defenseless body, but of a balanced, prosperous, and confident body: the body re-formed."

In each of the nine chapters, Clark traces how particular ideas and human motifs—Apollo-like reason, beauty, energy, pathos, and the like —have been represented through the nude since antiquity.

For example, he notes that in his work, *Temperance*, the fourteenth-century Italian sculptor Pisano "Christianized" the goddess Venus through "the turn and expression of the head. Instead of looking in the same direction as her body, and thus confirming her existence in the present, she turns and looks upward over her shoulder toward the promised world of the future...Giovanni Pisano had discovered a gesture that was to become the recognized expression of other-worldly longing." Hundreds of such insights bejewel the text.

To Clark, "the naked body is no more than the point of departure for a work of art." But what a "point of departure" it is! Unlike a landscape, say, it touches us directly as humans; we see ourselves in it. And its eroticism gives it just that extra tension that artists through the centuries have sought to transmute into higher feeling. Nudes sexy? Clark quotes one professor's scold that "if the nude is so treated that it raises in the spectator ideas or desires appropriate to the material subject, it is false art, and bad morals." Nonsense, says Clark, "No nude, however abstract, should fail to arouse in the spectator some vestige of erotic feeling...and if it does not do so, it is bad art and false morals."

In a sense, *The Nude* offers an erotically skewed course in the history of art. Are not most of the greats well-represented here? Polykleitos and Praxiteles are. So are Michelangelo and Botticelli, Picasso and Renoir, along with reproductions—298 of them—of their work. *The Nude* is like a perfect detail isolated from a larger canvas. ❖

# The Elements of Style

By William Strunk, Jr. and E. B. White
Earliest edition, by Strunk alone, appeared in 1918
First joint edition appeared in 1959

The world would be a better place if everybody read *The Elements of Style*; if it were read not just by writers and journalists, but by all who write legal briefs, job applications, love letters, or notes to the teacher; read even by those who never write anything. Even a single reading of the Strunk and White classic imparts at least temporary immunity to bureaucratic gobbledy-gook, technocratic jargon and psychobabble. If we all wrote and spoke clearly, without resort to weasel words and fuzzy generalities, maybe we'd all feel more at home with one another.

This is not too grand a judgment to make of so slim a book. *The Elements of Style* stands as a monument to clear thinking articulately voiced. Indeed, the terrible problem any writer faces in reviewing it is simply to live up to its injunctions. As the words click from the keyboard, he's apt to feel Messrs. Strunk and White peering over his shoulder, remarking on each empty phrase and murky thought.

William Strunk, Jr. was a Cornell professor who, back in 1918, had his little rule book on prose expression printed privately. A revised edition appeared in 1935. Twenty-two years later, a former student of Strunk, the noted essayist E. B. White, wrote a *New Yorker* piece about "my friend and teacher" Strunk and his book. In 1959, with that piece to serve as introduction, *The Elements of Style* reappeared with revisions, deletions, and a new chapter by White. This is the edition better known today as "Strunk and White" than by its formal title.

White's charming introductory tribute to Strunk leads off this guidebook. It is followed by a chapter on rules of usage, another on principles of composition, and a concise rundown of "Words and Expressions Commonly Misused." The final chapter is White's own "Approach to Style," advanced through Strunkian rules such as "Do not affect a breezy manner," and "Write with nouns and verbs."

None of this, of course, hints at the sparkling clarity here; it is a delight to read, and for the first-time reader, may be experienced as revealed wisdom. "Prefer the specific to the general," is the essential Strunk speaking. For example, he says, the sentence "He showed satisfaction as he took possession of his well-earned reward" just won't do; much better is "He grinned as he pocketed the coin." And we grin in recognition of Truth.

In the clear, crystalline world of Strunk and White, acts of a hostile character become *hostile acts*. The phrase *in the last analysis* is "bankrupt"; the word *interesting* is "unconvincing...Instead of announcing that what you are about to tell is interesting, make it so." As for an occasional colloquialism, "simply use it; do not draw attention to it by enclosing it in quotation marks. To do so is to put on airs, as though you were inciting the reader to join you in a select society of those who know better."

The final chapter on writing style displays all White's own mastery of the essay form. "Writing," he says, "becomes a question of learning to make occasional wing shots, bringing down the bird of thought as it flashes by. A writer is a gunner, sometimes waiting in his blind for something to come in, sometimes roaming the countryside hoping to scare something up." Then come twenty-one of White's own rules, echoing the voice of his mentor—as when he describes words like *rather, very, little, pretty* as "leeches that infest the pond of prose, sucking the blood of words."

One paragraph appears twice within *The Elements of Style*. Originally penned by Strunk in advancing his dictum to "omit needless words," White repeats it verbatim in his introduction. Here it is:

" 'Vigorous writing is concise. A sentence should contain no unnecessary words, a paragraph no unnecessary sentences, for the same reason that a drawing should have no unnecessary lines and a machine no unnecessary parts. This requires not that the writer make all his sentences short, or that he avoid all detail and treat his subjects only in outline, but that every word tell.'

"There you have a short, valuable essay on the nature and beauty of brevity," wrote White. "Sixty-three words that could change the world." ❖

# EIGHT

# One-of-a-Kinds

| | |
|---|---|
| *A Room of One's Own* | Virginia Woolf |
| *The American Language* | H. L. Mencken |
| *The Little Prince* | Antoine de Saint Exupéry |
| *The Education of Henry Adams* | Henry Adams |
| *Flatland* | Edwin A. Abbott |
| *Their Eyes Were Watching God* | Zora Neale Hurston |
| *A Mathematician's Apology* | G. H. Hardy |
| *My Life* | Isadora Duncan |
| *The Structure of Scientific Revolutions* | Thomas Kuhn |

Some books that *could* be seen as falling under some other category nonetheless seem unique—absolutely distinctive, one-of-a-kind. Whether by virtue of the idea that drives it, as in *Flatland,* or the peculiar voice that marks it, as in *The Education of Henry Adams*, or by the sheer power of its argument, as in *The Structure of Scientific Revolutions*, none of these books could ever be mistaken for any other.

# A Room of One's Own

### By Virginia Woolf
### First published in 1929

In October, 1928, at the age of forty-seven, the great English novelist and essayist Virginia Woolf was asked to give a series of lectures on the subject "Women and Fiction." Now, imagine that subject in the hands of your garden-variety pedagogue. Imagine the tired theorizing, the labored academic posturing, the gray tide of literary references. And imagine such a discourse's likely effects upon the hapless listeners.

By a brilliant lecturer, the talk might conceivably turn out provocative, even profound. But downright pleasurable? A sheer delight? Enchanting?

That is just what Woolf accomplished—an outcome recorded in the expanded written version of her talk, *A Room of One's Own.*

As it happens, she did so using a literary device that foreshadows one Norman Mailer would use forty years later in *The Armies of the Night*, his account of the 1967 March on the Pentagon. Mailer employed a third-person version of himself—"Mailer," he called him—to portray the action. Through this "Mailer's" eyes the reader viewed the massive war protest; through "Mailer's" perceptions, he came to see its meaning. "History as a novel, the novel as history," the author called the resulting form.

In *A Room of One's Own* Woolf foreswore the third person, but the effect is similarly compelling. "I propose," she says right off, to make "use of all the liberties and licenses of a novelist to tell you the story of the two days that preceded my coming here—how, bowed down by the weight of the subject which you have laid upon my shoulders, I pondered it, and made it work in and out of my daily life. I need not say," she goes on, "that what I am about to describe has no existence...'I' is only a convenient term for somebody who has no real being...Call me Mary Beton, Mary Seton, Mary Carpenter"—all earlier women writers with whom she felt a bond.

"A woman," Woolf writes before properly beginning her "story," "must have money and a room of her own if she is to write fiction." Then she proceeds to illuminate the process by which she arrived at that conclusion.

As protagonist of her intellectual tale, she lolls upon the banks of a river, wondering how best to approach her subject. She strolls through courts and quadrangles of the great university she calls Oxbridge, pondering Milton and Thackeray. She leaves Oxbridge for London, wondering, "Why did men drink wine and women water? Why was one sex so prosperous and the other so poor? What effect has poverty on fiction? What conditions are necessary for the creation of works of art?"

She visits the British Museum, leafs through tomes men have written on the subject of women, like one by a German professor on "The Mental, Moral, and Physical Inferiority of the Female Sex." She ponders the fate of Shakespeare's sister, asking what became of her genius while Will was hanging out with the boys at the Globe. She samples novels by women from earliest times to the then-present, pointing up this one's strengths, that one's weaknesses, setting both against the oppressive constraints under which all women worked.

But always, giving life to her thesis, is her little story: "Next day," after returning from the museum, she writes, "the light of the October morning was falling in dusty shafts through the uncurtained windows, and the hum of traffic rose from the street. London then was winding itself up again." And each of these "scenes"—though so slight in contribution to "plot" they scarcely deserve the name—advances the line of her argument a little further.

It is, I must tell you, tempting to ignore the substance of that argument and focus wholly on its maker—to go off starry-eyed at having passed hours in the company of this masterful stylist. A contemporary critic apparently had the same idea when the book first came out: "What matters her argument," he wrote, "providing she keeps writing books like these."

Woolf's is not a Spartan, clippity-clop style such as the one Ernest Hemingway was perfecting in Paris at about the same time. This is leisurely, ruminative, with long paragraphs that march up and down the page, long trains of thought, and rich digressions almost hypnotic in their effect. And once trapped within the sweet, sticky filament of her web of words, one is left with no wish whatever to be set free. ❖

ROBERT KANIGEL

# The American Language:
## An Inquiry into the Development of English in the United States

By H. L. Mencken
First published in 1919
Revisions and supplements through 1948

H. L. Mencken never wrote anything that wasn't a delight to read. And *The American Language*—a footnoted, indexed, annotated, exhaustively researched philology text, for God's sake!—is no exception. It begins with an essay, on the centuries-old linguistic warfare between the snooty British and the endlessly inventive Americans, that has no business being anything but incorrigibly dull. Except it's not; it's fascinating and fun.

Mencken's subject is American English, what distinguishes it from that spoken and written in the mother country, the way its development mirrored the country's own, its glorious Wild West excesses, the debt it owes America's Indians and immigrants, and much more. Spelling and pronunciation, slang, grammar and proper names each draw Mencken's attention. In all, several thousand words receive at least a passing note, and often substantially more, on their etymology, pronunciation, or usage.

Did you know that Thomas Jefferson first coined "to belittle," a word that became the subject of mockery among the educated classes on the other side of the Atlantic?

Or that "Salisbury steak," a staple of cafeterias everywhere, is a holdover from World War I, when anything so remotely German as a hamburger carried a tinge of treason?

Or that long before "prioritize" came along to reduce today's defenders of the English pure to apoplexy, Americans were using "electrize" (meaning to electrocute), "sloganize," and "backwardize?" And that good ol' everyday "burglarize" goes back only to 1871?

Did you know that the kind of crude cigar known as a "stogy" goes back to the "Conestoga," the classic covered wagon of pioneer fame, which in turn derived from a valley in Lancaster County, Pa., named for an extinct band of Iroquois Indians?

Mencken, who owned what at the time was the best private linguistics library in the United States, is full of stuff like that. And in virtually every paragraph he exhibits the very insouciance he ascribes to American English itself. Here's Mencken on dictionary-maker Noah Webster: "It was almost impossible for him to imagine himself in error, and most of his disquisitions were far more pontifical than argumentative in tone. He had no respect for dignity or authority...When it came to whooping up his spelling-book he was completely shameless, and did not hesitate to demand encomiums from Washington, Jefferson and Franklin."

Don't you wish they had written your high school history text that way?

Or listen to Mencken lace into Walt Whitman: "His early prose was dingy, cliche-laden journalese of the era, and after his discovery of Carlyle he indulged himself in a heavy imitation of the Scotsman's gnarled and tortured style. Not many specimens of the popular speech ever got into his writings, either in prose or in verse. He is remembered for few besides 'yawp' and 'gawk.' His own inventions were mainly cacophonous miscegenations of roots and suffixes, e.g. 'Scientism,' 'presidentiat,' 'venerealese'..., and not one of them has ever gained any currency."

It was through intellectual panzer attacks like that, of course, that Mencken made his name; the New York Times once called him "the most powerful private citizen in America." But this book owes as much to his delight in the linguistic exuberance of his compatriots as to his contempt for the philologists and "school ma'ams" of his generation. Indeed, if you want to feel irretrievably and proudly American, read Mencken and realize how many words and expressions in daily use have their roots in our soil:

"Bum a ride," or have your hair "styled" by a "beautician," or "letter" in a sport, or "research" a book, or "bulldoze" a house for a "superhighway," or take a "lengthy" vacation, or endure a "hot spell," or rummage at the "bargain counter" of a "department store," or even claim "mileage" deductions on your income tax return, and you're using Americanisms—"dyed-in-the-wool" Americanisms at that.

Mencken loved our language. *The American Language* is a work of high scholarship infused and enriched by that love. ❖

# The Little Prince

*By Antoine de Saint Exupéry*
*First published in 1943*

If there were taboos against ridiculing grown-ups as there are against ethnic minorities, *The Little Prince* might never have been published. Adults are an absurd and unimaginative lot, one comes away from it convinced. One best avoids them. And, at all costs, one avoids growing up into one. Among representatives of the species we meet in Antoine de Saint Exupéry's classic are:

- An alcoholic who drinks to forget his shame over drinking.

- A king who expects instant obedience from his subjects, of whom he has none.

- A businessman who occupies himself by toting up his possessions, which consist of the stars in the sky; they are his, he explains, because it was he who first thought to own them.

- A man who wears a hat just so he can tip it in acknowledgement of admiring comments.

These characters inhabit small planets visited by the little prince in trips through the galaxy after leaving his own planet. Finally, reaching Earth, he meets the narrator, an aviator (like Saint Exupéry himself) whose plane has broken down and crashed in the Sahara.

The narrator, we learn, once nourished hopes of becoming an artist. But as a child, he was discouraged by grown-ups who failed to see in the amoeboid shape he drew with a colored pencil what was so plain to him —a boa constrictor consuming an elephant. Advised to lay aside his drawings and turn instead to history, arithmetic and grammar, he'd done so. Now, his plane wrecked in the desert, he encounters the little prince, with his flowing scarf, his love of sunsets, his haunting innocence.

The planet of this little prince was one he'd shared with three volcanoes (one of them extinct), occasional growths of baobab tree roots (which must be uprooted lest they grow and split the planet into pieces), a few caterpillars and a single flower. This flower was coquettish, willful and not entirely likable—a flower with perhaps the most complex personality in all of literature.

Spurned by the flower, the little prince had left his own world and begun his planet-hopping travels. On Earth, he'd met a fox who'd reminded him of the eternal verities of life that grown-ups have forgotten and are too busy to relearn. They "set out on their way in express trains," the little prince says of adults, "but they do not know what they are looking for. Then they rush about, and get excited, and turn round and round."

None of this, I hasten to add, is silly. It is far more serious, for example, than stock quotations from Wall Street. Children will instantly grasp its significance. Even adults inclined to say, like the star-owning businessman, "I don't amuse myself with balderdash," will catch on. To be left unmoved by *The Little Prince* is to be a lump of asphalt.

But please, whatever you do, don't let the Adult Anti-Defamation Commission get its imagination-starved mitts on it. Just as kings and presidents invoke the specter of The Enemy around which to unite the masses, Saint Exupéry rallies his readers against adults. Or rather, against the constellation of traits that usually emerge once past childhood and make us into the literal-minded, pompous and vain creatures we are.

Indeed, the author goes so far as to apologize to his readers for dedicating the book to his friend, a grown-up, then actually corrects the dedication to read: "To Leon Werth—when he was a little boy."

*The Little Prince* is a book to read when you can't recall the last time you drew pictures in the sand, played ping-pong with a porpoise, raced the minute hand to twelve, or floated in a raft to the moon. ❖

ROBERT KANIGEL

# The Education of Henry Adams

*By Henry Adams*
*First published in 1918, after a private printing in 1906*

Nephew of a Harvard president, grandson of a U.S. president and great-grandson of another, Henry Adams was the son of the American ambassador to England, Charles Francis Adams. At the age of twenty-three, he served his father in London as personal secretary and watched up close as Adams senior, in a heroic bout of Civil War diplomacy, kept England neutral despite its sympathies for the South. Adams emerged later as among the most distinguished historians of his time. He was a world traveler and world figure, counting many of America's and Britain's intellectual elite among his friends and acquaintances.

And yet, in *The Education of Henry Adams*, Adams comes across as almost pathologically diffident. If you didn't know better, you might conclude he knew nothing and learned less, that his life was directionless, his judgment unerringly wrong. You might so conclude, that is, until you remembered that Adams enjoyed the company of the nineteenth century's literary, intellectual, and political giants; and that *The Education* was first circulated privately to only about a hundred intimates—none of whom needed the slightest reminder of his achievements.

Adams' diffidence served a rhetorical purpose—to argue that by upbringing, schooling, travel, early life experiences, and training, his "education"—as well as those of his whole generation—left him unprepared for the complex world into which he was thrust. Adams' great-grandfather, John Adams, succeeded George Washington as president in 1797. Adams himself lived to see World War I; he finished *The Education* about when Einstein was polishing up his theory of relativity, when bicycles, automobiles, and telephones were everywhere, and with world affairs descending into chaos. This new world, Adams says on every page, was one for which his education left him unfit.

Adams' account includes perfect little sketches of key nineteenth-century figures, like Swinburne, Garibaldi, the abolitionist senator Charles Sumner, and Adams' close friend John Hay, secretary of state under McKinley and Theodore Roosevelt and author of the Open Door policy to China. Similarly evocative are portraits of Chicago, Berlin, London, Paris, Rome: "In 1860 the lights and shadows were still medieval, and medieval Rome was alive; the shadows breathed and glowed, full of soft forms felt by lost senses. No sand-blast of science had yet skinned off the epidermis of history, thought and feeling. The pictures were uncleaned, the churches unrestored, the ruins unexcavated."

But all this merely establishes context for Adams' confusion at finding himself in a coal-fired age of dynamos, ocean steamers, and an imperially-minded America. Even seemingly innocuous bits of travelogue serve his point: "Rome," he concludes, "was the worst spot on earth to teach nineteenth-century youth what to do with a twentieth-century world."

This is an intellectual autobiography, an account of what Adams came to think and how he came to think it. His public life is well represented. His sometimes wearisome notions of history as a dynamic force get full vent. But his personal life intrudes hardly at all. Wholly absent are the two decades of his life before 1892. During that period, he wrote two novels (under a pseudonym); married; bore the death of his father and the suicide of his wife by cyanide poisoning; commissioned the distinguished sculptor Augustus St. Gaudens to make a monument to his wife that now stands in Rock Creek Cemetery in Washington; and wrote his monumental nine-volume history of the Jefferson and Madison administrations. All this gets but the sketchiest mention. "What one did—or did not do—with one's education, after getting it," Adams insists, "need trouble the inquirer in no way; it is a personal matter only which would confuse him."

So *The Education* is a curious amalgam. While outwardly autobiographical, it leaves long periods of the author's life untouched. While offering insight into nineteenth-century international diplomacy, it cites the historical record itself only obliquely, leaving one scurrying to other sources. While revealing the play of Adams' mind, it hides almost the whole of his heart.

To the modern reader, its importance lies in making more comprehensible the great middle period of the American experiment. No longer will the reader see the Revolutionary, Civil, Spanish-American, and First World Wars as merely violent exclamation points, connected only by sodden text in a history book. It is as if Henry Adams had taken a needle and, through his own life and that of his family, stitched a continuous thread between the nation's beginnings in the eighteenth century and its coming of age in the twentieth. ❖

# Flatland

## A Romance of Many Dimensions

*By Edwin A. Abbott*
*First published in 1884*

You and I live in three dimensions. The would-be author of *Flatland*, identified in the original edition only as "a Square," lives in two. His tale—a lively, provocative blend of science fiction, pure mathematics and social satire—recounts his discovery of the third dimension, and his fate at the hands of fellow Flatlanders for daring to tell about it.

*Flatland* could so easily have been just another clever idea amateurishly executed, like a sophomore's strained efforts at "creative" writing; instead, it's a virtuoso performance. Imagined details of its world are worked out with great clarity and precision. The range of human social experience upon which it comments is astounding.

The basics: In Flatland, the universe is a thin disc of limitless extent. We, in Spaceland, can look down upon the otherwise quite human triangles, squares, and hexagons who inhabit it. But confined to their pancake of a world, Flatlanders themselves can't see one another, though they can infer presences.

In Flatland's pecking order, status rises with the number of one's sides. Thus, Triangles are lowly, Pentagons higher, and infinitely-sided Circles highest of all, forming a priestly caste. The author is a Square, a professional or gentleman. Equilateral Triangles are sturdy yeomen. Below them lies an underclass of brutish Isosceles Triangles, some, of greater "irregularity" than others, being scarcely civilized at all. And the lowest of the low, subject to special rules of behavior, and not polygons at all but merely straight lines with heads and tails? Why, women, of course.

How do Flatlanders, restricted to their paper-thin plane of existence and able to discern only edges and lines, recognize one another? In just one example of an imaginative device doing double duty as technical expedient and social commentary, they have available three means—Hearing, Feeling and Sight Recognition—their reliance on each depending on their social station. Thus, "feeling" roughly corresponds to the crude physicality often attributed to peasant cultures, while "sight recognition" is the lofty pursuit of the upper classes.

Author Edwin A. Abbott's ironies are so gentle, and seem to arise so organically from his world, it's as if he were slyly saying, "Oh, does that conjure up some conceit or frailty of your own society? Well, now, what a coincidence..." He exhibits almost Machiavellian clearsightedness about how societies are constituted, neither lacking compassion for the oppressed nor becoming overwrought about them.

Thus, in Abbot's world, Isosceles Triangles of the lowest orders occasionally beget better endowed Equilateral Triangles. Not surprisingly, this occasions rejoicing among them—but satisfaction, too, among the aristocracy; for here is a safe, slow means of upward mobility that neither weakens their control nor diminishes their privileges—a "most useful barrier against revolution."

All of this is good satire, good science fiction, good geometry. But Abbott takes it further yet: In the final moments of the Flatland calendar's twentieth century—corresponding, in other words, to its Millennium—our hero, our modest, two-dimensional Square, is granted a revelation:

"Straightaway I became conscious of a Presence in the room, and a chilling breath thrilled through my very being," he writes. A priestly Circle appears in his home, unbidden, shimmering with an otherworldly glow, growing larger or smaller seemingly at will. This, he learns, is no ordinary Circle, but rather part of a great Sphere sectioned through by Flatland.

Through him—Him?—our Square learns of a third dimension beyond his own. Lifted into space, he's treated to the rich panorama of a universe he'd previously experienced only as lines and edges. His mind stretched beyond its Flatland limits, he begins to preach the Gospel of Three Dimensions, of an elusive, higher world Flatlanders never see... Thus, abruptly, satire and science fiction yield to what we today call "higher consciousness."

The author, an English theologian whose hobby was mathematics, created in Flatland a world. Within its narrow confines, he succeeded in commenting upon his own world, and ours. ❖

# Their Eyes Were Watching God

*By Zora Neale Hurston*
*First published in 1937*

"He look like some ole skullhead in de grave yard."

That's how Janie Crawford, a young black woman growing up in western Florida, describes the older man her nanny wants to make her marry and for whom she cares nothing. So when big Jody Starks comes along, full of button-popping ambition and big plans for moving down to Eatonville, where black people are building a town of their own, she joins him. She aches to love and to experience wider vistas, and Jody supplies one if not the other: "He did not represent sun-up and pollen and blooming trees, but he spoke for far horizon."

In Eatonville, Jody becomes mayor and starts a general store that becomes a focal point of the town's life. And there, on the store's front porch, much of the broad middle section of Zora Neale Hurston's novel, *Their Eyes Were Watching God*, takes place. There the local men congregate of an evening to trade stories, insults and gossip. There they toy with poor Matt Bonner and the mule he fairly starves.

"Dat mule uh yourn, Matt. You better go see 'bout him. He's bad off."

"Where 'bouts? Did he wade in de lake and uh alligator ketch him?"

"Worser'n dat. De womenfolks got yo' mule. When ah come round de lake 'bout noontime mah wife and some others has 'im flat on de ground usin' his side fuh uh wash board."

Some, conceivably, may feel embarrassed to see this rural dialect reduced to print, with no attempt to metamorphose it into English that is correct, grammatical—and white. But this novel, so full of dignity and strength, needs no excuses made on its behalf. Its characters are well drawn and distinct; some are foolish, some possess intelligence and grace. They may speak like Amos 'n' Andy, but the comparison ends there. Like William Faulkner, Hurston—a figure in that flowering of black culture and consciousness between the world wars known as the Harlem Renaissance—evokes the rich cultural roots of outwardly simple rural life.

Janie is not quite a "strong" woman, as we use the word today. She still largely depends on men and does what they expect her to do, whether running the store as Jody demands, or working in the fields as Tea Cake, her first real love, wishes. Still, she never merely settles, at least not permanently. And never for the sadly constrained life her Nanny, a former slave, has schooled her to accept. Instead, she clings to the vision that life can be fuller and richer. She finds such a life with the playful Tea Cake.

Outwardly, she conforms, but always consciously, knowingly. When Jody dies, she dons black and bears herself as a widow should. But then, too soon for the town's tastes, she meets Tea Cake and takes to dressing in bright colors.

"Ah ain't grievin' so why do Ah hafta mourn?" she says to Phoeby, a friend who warns her of wagging tongues. "Tea Cake love me in blue, so Ah wears it. Jody ain't never in his life picked out no color for me. De world picked out black and white for mournin', Joe didn't. So Ah wasn't wearing it for him. Ah was wearin' it for de rest of y'all."

Hurston speaks in two voices: in the dialect of her characters, and in a narrator's voice clear, correct, and lush with poetry. When Jody upbraids Janie for a flash of independence—it's *his* job to think for women, children, chickens and cows—she withdraws: "The bed was no longer a daisy-field for her and Joe to play in. It was a place where she went and laid down when she was sleepy and tired. She wasn't petal-open anymore with him."

Later, a hurricane stirs in the Everglades: "The monster began to roll in his bed. Began to roll and complain like a peevish world on a grumble."

That "monster" ultimately tramples across the sunny, green field of Janie's new life, and once again she must start over, returning to Eatonville. "Ah'm back home agin and Ah'm satisfied tuh be heah," she tells Phoeby. "Ah done been tuh de horizon." ❖

# A Mathematician's Apology

*By G. H. Hardy*
*First published in 1940*

Pity the poor mathematician stuck working out some problem in chemistry, ballistics, or other dreary subject, says G. H. Hardy, author of this eloquent defense of pure mathematics; for the sheer utility of the work strands him from all that is mathematically loveliest. " 'Imaginary' universes are so much more beautiful than this stupidly constructed 'real' one," he writes, "and most of the finest products of an applied mathematician's fancy must be rejected, as soon as they have been created, for the brutal but sufficient reason that they do not fit the facts."

For Hardy, the leading English mathematician of the early part of this century, known both for his own achievements and for introducing Indian mathematical prodigy Srinivasa Ramanujan to Cambridge University and the West, mathematics bore no relation to the tedium of long division we remember from grammar school; nor the angled ladders of high school trigonometry; nor the indefinite integrals memorized for college calculus.

No, for him mathematics was an art form, one demanding the same resources of creativity required of a composer or poet. (One review of *A Mathematician's Apology* when it first appeared called it one of the best accounts of what being a creative artist was all about. The review was by novelist Graham Greene, who ought to know.) "There is no permanent place in the world for ugly mathematics," writes Hardy, in a typically aesthetics-rooted assertion. "A mathematical proof should resemble a simple and clear-cut constellation, not a scattered cluster in the Milky Way."

In rhetorical tradition, an "apology" like Hardy's is a formal defense of an idea, institution, or work; in this case, even more than most, the word means nothing like what it does in everyday speech. Hardy's spirited argument reveals neither defensiveness nor diffidence. If anything, it verges on arrogance, full of cheerful mathematical chauvinism as when Hardy says that the mathematician "Archimedes will be remembered when Aeschylus is forgotten, because languages die and mathematical ideas do not."

The whole long essay is like that, shot through with the serene assurance that pure mathematics is a noble endeavor. He abjures every superficially appealing and familiar defense of mathematics—that it is useful, that it does human good, and the like—and throws the weight of his argument on the very claim perhaps most difficult to sustain before a lay readership, that mathematics is beautiful.

What makes for beauty in a mathematical proof? Hardy offers simple examples from Euclid and Pythagoras that, he feels, exhibit a "high degree of *unexpectedness*, combined with *inevitability* and *economy*." All three qualities, it need hardly be added, apply as well to other aesthetic realms, including writing. And all three qualities apply to *A Mathematician's Apology*. Hardy's readiness to dismiss the utility of mathematics is surely unexpected. And the book's whole argument, though well-developed, is succinct, proceeding as if in response to natural law. For one with such a head for number and symbol, Hardy certainly has an ear for words—giving us the opportunity to taste through language what few of us can appreciate in mathematics itself.

In his foreword to the 1967 edition, English novelist C. P. Snow, a long-time younger friend of Hardy, asks us to see the *Apology* "as a book of desperate sadness," the product of a mathematician long past his creative prime. "It is a melancholy experience for a professional mathematician to find himself writing about mathematics," writes Hardy. As an old man now, washed up as a mathematician, writing about mathematics, he comes close to saying, is all that's left him.

But might Snow have been fooled by Hardy's rhetorical flourishes? Or, more likely, by knowing Hardy, the man, too well in the years before his death? The sadness in the *Apology* is there all right, but more as the resignation accompanying a rich, full life inevitably nearing its end, than the bitter reflection of a life poorly spent. The overall feeling is one of satisfaction, not despair; of fullness, not the void. ❖

# My Life

*By Isadora Duncan*
*First published in 1927*

"Just as there are days when my life seems to have been a Golden Legend studded with precious jewels, a flowery field with multitudes of blossoms, a radiant morn with love and happiness crowning every hour... so there are other days when, trying to recollect my life, I am filled only with a great disgust and a feeling of utter emptiness."

That's how much of this autobiography of Isadora Duncan reads— with grandiloquence and passion. Judged on narrow standards of literary merit alone, it might be dismissed easily. Yet somehow, for *this* author, we must make allowances...Imagine a lone figure on the stage, barefoot, garbed only in a simple white Greek tunic, her body flowing to the swelling sound of Wagner's "The Ride of the Valkyries." This is the great Isadora. Her native language is dance, not English prose. But many a reader will willingly suffer three hundred pages of it for the chance to come under her spell.

It's a bargain, one suspects, like many struck with her during her lifetime—when friends, lovers, fellow artists and impresarios endured her excesses and idiosyncrasies, her narcissism and her single-mindedness, for the chance to touch the soul of one of the most distinctive personalities of the twentieth century.

Born in 1878, Duncan was raised in San Francisco but spent most of her dance career in Europe. She regarded herself as a genius; she was certainly one of a kind. She rejected classical ballet, which she viewed as unnatural and silly. She dismissed jazz and the dance it inspired, popular at the time she wrote, as barbaric. She favored instead a free and natural dance movement inspired by classical Greek forms.

Her life was as distinctive as her art. She was the honored guest of millionaires. She rebuffed the sexual advances of sculptor Auguste Rodin —only later to sweep aside her Puritan past and take numerous lovers, few of whom she describes in *My Life* as anything less than geniuses. On landing in Greece, she kissed its sacred earth. She and her brother Raymond, as romantic as she, set about building a Greek temple near Athens—a project they had to give up when they realized there was no fresh water for miles around.

Later, at the height of her fame, having impressed her genius on the world, she lost much of what gave meaning to her life on a country road outside Paris. There, her two children, born to different men, neither of whom she married, died in an apparent—it's not quite clear from the text —automobile accident. Now she was no longer the great Isadora; she was a mother in agony.

Duncan was sure her approach to dance would, as she told one famous dancer, "revolutionize our entire epoch." She had discovered it, she wrote, "by the Pacific Ocean, by the waving pine-forests of Sierra Nevada. I have seen the ideal figure of youthful America dancing over the top of the Rockies...I have discovered the dance that is worthy of the poems of Walt Whitman..."

*My Life* is one flourish like that after another, appeals to Art, Beauty and Truth fairly tumbling from the page, its author seemingly unmindful of how a steady diet of impassioned outpourings might affect her readers. Structurally, the book is a weakly linked chain of travels, performances, love affairs, money problems and devoted audiences held in her thrall.

It would be easy to write off all this as the ravings of a wild-eyed visionary, and to sneer at sensibilities that, at least on paper, lack all subtlety. On the other hand, we get a chance to see up close just the kind of intense and uninhibited personal vision—the supreme egotism, the sense of her own mission—from which many artists draw. Even as she scandalized the folks back home with her personal life, Duncan was the toast of

Europe—a fact she delights in recounting through lengthy quotes from flattering reviews.

We glimpse in this flawed account some of what Isadora might have been like as a dancer. We sense her raw, uninhibited energy. We feel her life force. ❖

# The Structure of Scientific Revolutions

### By Thomas S. Kuhn
### First appeared in 1962

By close study of rocks or trees, atoms or stars, scientists draw conclusions about how the world is made. From firm, neutral facts, they construct theories, then test them against new data. Gradually, over years and centuries, theory is bent to accommodate new evidence. And imperceptibly, like bricks fitted into a wall, science's picture of the universe takes new form.

This, roughly, is the conventional view of how science progresses. But it bears almost no relation to how science really does progress. Or so said Thomas Kuhn in *The Structure of Scientific Revolutions*; on its appearance almost forty years ago, he changed, virtually overnight, how many saw science working.

Kuhn could scarcely have imagined the reception his long essay would receive. Issued by a university publisher as part of a series (the other two dozen volumes of which remain largely obscure) the book, now in its third edition, has sold upwards of six hundred thousand copies. Each year, hundreds of scholarly treatises cite it. One publisher came out with a collection of essays devoted exclusively to issues it raised. And while, narrowly speaking, the book deals only with the physical sciences, its ideas are, as one critic has put it, "so seductive" that scholars in economics, political science and sociology have applied them to their own fields.

What *really* happens in science, said Thomas Kuhn, is that some long-prevailing view of nature undergoes, abruptly and disconcertingly, a "paradigm shift"—a revolution in form not so different from a political one. Einstein, said Kuhn, changed the way we see the world: Relativity theory changed the kinds of experiments scientists perform, the instruments they use, the form of the questions they ask, even the types of problems considered important. Einstein ushered in a revolution. So did Newton, Lavoisier, Dalton.

While the old paradigm yet prevails, "normal science" is the rule. This he defines as "research firmly based upon one or more past scientific achievements…that some particular scientific community acknowledges for a time as supplying the foundation for its further practice."

The practitioners of normal science don't run around, willy-nilly, gathering stray bits of data. Rather, all they do is based on some prior scientific pattern—for example, the phlogiston theory of combustion, or Newtonian dynamics, or relativity theory. They seek particular kinds of facts, to fit particular gaps of knowledge, employing particular kinds of scientific apparatus. Moreover, as Kuhn writes, "other problems (than those the paradigm deems relevant) are rejected as metaphysical, as the concern of another discipline, or sometimes as just too problematic to be worth the time. A paradigm can even insulate the community from… socially important problems."

Now this paradigm, whatever it is, is logically self-contained. It explains past experimental results. It leads to the successful solution of new problems. But from time to time, discrepancies arise. In the end, most of these "anomalous" results are successfully explained away or otherwise dismissed. But some are shoved into a back corner of the scientific enterprise, there to nag the minds of a few.

With enough such anomalous results, the particular science may be thrown into crisis. Theories contend. And the contending theories are not just mildly differing interpretations but radically different views of nature. They are—to use another of the half-dozen words that Kuhn's essay gave a special flavor—"incommensurable." Finally, out of this clash of theories is built a new scientific order, a new paradigm that all but die-hard champions of the old paradigm accept.

Kuhn cites a classic psychological experiment from the 1940s: An experimenter briefly flashes upon a screen images of playing cards and asks the subject to say what he sees. Every so often, a black four of hearts, say, is substituted for the normal red one. At first, the subject is oblivious to the switch, continuing to see the kinds of cards for which all his previous experience prepared him. The conventional deck is his paradigm, the altered cards the anomaly he subconsciously dismisses. Ultimately, as exposure time to the cards increases, he may sense something wrong, perhaps experiencing great distress: He cannot discard his paradigm lightly.

Neither can scientists. But when they do, a wonderful moment arrives in the intellectual life of our species. ❖

# The Realm of the Spirit

### Holy and Human

| | |
|---|---|
| *Gilgamesh* | Babylonian epic |
| *Confessions* | Saint Augustine |
| *The Golem* | Gustav Meyrink |
| *The Razor's Edge* | W. Somerset Maugham |
| *The Seven Storey Mountain* | Thomas Merton |
| *Death Be Not Proud* | John Gunther |
| *Ecclesiastes* | Old Testament |
| *Lost Horizon* | James Hilton |
| *The Bhagavad Gita* | Sanskrit poem |
| *Night* | Elie Wiesel |
| *The Varieties of Religious Experience* | William James |

---

Is there a God? Where is He when evil comes? Can the rational and logically reductive explain all that needs explaining, or do spiritual realms stand beside those of the intellect, revealing their own truths? What is the purpose of life? How ought we to live and die?

It's easy to dismiss such questions as beyond us, or else laugh them off as the stuff of *Peanuts* cartoons. But sometimes, in the soul's dark night, we seek answers—and in these books, ancient and more recent, may perhaps find them.

# *Gilgamesh*

*Babylonian epic dating to
as early as the third millennium B.C.*

Gilgamesh is king in Babylonia, a brutal tyrant who has squandered any respect or love his people ever had for him. Into his life comes Enkidu, a half animal/half human nursed into manhood by a prostitute.

One day the king comes to town to select a temple virgin as his bed partner, only to find Enkidu blocking the way, acclaimed as new champion of the people.

*They fell like wolves
At each other's throats,
Like bulls bellowing,
And horses gasping for breath
That have run all day
Desperate for rest and water*

But mysteriously, amid their struggle, they pause, look into each other's eyes, and see some irreducible part of themselves alive in the other.

They become friends. Together they venture forth to kill Humbaba, powerful lord of the cedar forest. Each gives the other strength and will that, for the moment, the other may lack. In the end, the head of Humbaba is left swinging from a tree.

The goddess Ishtar, whose marriage proposal Gilgamesh has spurned, turns bitterly to her father, demanding a heavenly bull wreak revenge on humankind in general and Gilgamesh in particular. But Enkidu kills the bull, hurling its thigh bone back at the enraged Ishtar.

The gods decree that one of them, Gilgamesh or Enkidu, must die, and Enkidu wakes from a dream realizing it must be he. Weakened by his wounds, he slips away...

*Gilgamesh knew his friend was close to death.*
*He tried to recollect aloud their life together*
*That had been so brief, so empty of gestures*
*They never felt they had to make. Tears filled his own eyes*

And here a story, at first blush a paean to the mindless violence and strutting of a barbarous age, seems transmuted, in the love between these two men, into something softer, gentler, more *modern*. Enkidu does die. Gilgamesh is left inconsolable, his grief so prolonged and sharp that no one who has felt cheated by similar loss can soon forget it.

*Gilgamesh wept bitterly for his friend.*
*He felt himself now singled out for loss*
*Apart from everyone else. The word Enkidu*
*Roamed through every thought*
*Like a hungry animal through empty lairs*
*In search of food. The only nourishment*
*He knew was grief, endless in its hidden source*
*Yet never ending hunger.*

With Enkidu's death, the tone of the story shifts once more, now becoming a kind of spiritual mystery. For Gilgamesh doesn't passively accept the death of his friend. Rather, he sets out to overturn the verdict rendered by the gods, venturing off alone into the country of the dead, trying to restore Enkidu to life.

This, then, is the story that comes down to us through text chiseled into stone tablets, unearthed in the last century from ruins in Nineveh, in

Mesopotamia. (The verse transcribed above, by Herbert Mason, represents only one of many translations available, most of them much more literal.)

Gilgamesh displays no stiff upper lip in the face of his friend's death. Many a therapist of today might judge the intensity of his response "inappropriate"; might suggest that, after some due period of mourning, he pick up the pieces of his life, set grief aside. Those of more guarded emotions, meanwhile, might even judge the intensity of his response unseemly or undignified.

And yet, for me, it is Gilgamesh's response to the death of his friend that seems more authentic, more true to human nature, than the store-bought funeral etiquette of today that demands austere dignity in the face of loss too terrible to bear. ❖

# Confessions

*By Saint Augustine*
*First appeared in 398 A.D.*

Is there reason for any but a Christian theologian to read these *Confessions* of Aurelius Augustinus, whom the Catholic Church later called a saint? Are they more than just a long, extended prayer fit for a distinguished place in the religious literature and nowhere else?

Augustine was born in North Africa in 354 A.D., son of a philandering, pagan father and pious Christian mother. Both strains run deep in him: The *Confessions* hold interest for modern, secular readers largely in the tension between the two warring elements of his nature.

In his lusty, irrepressible youth, his father's example plainly ruled him. "I liked to score a fine win at sport or to have my ears tickled by the make-believe of the stage, which only made them itch the more. As time went on my eyes shone more and more with the same eager curiosity, because I wanted to see the shows and sports which grown-ups enjoyed."

Later, adult temptations proved equally irresistible. He succumbed frequently to the embrace of women. He may also have had at least one homosexual liaison; Augustine is not clear on the point, saying only that his relationship to a male friend "was sweeter to me than all the joys of life as I lived it then." When his friend died, he grieved, even contemplated suicide: "I felt that our two souls had been as one, living in two bodies, and life to me was fearful because I did not want to live with half a soul."

(Even after his conversion to Christianity when he was thirty-three, he confesses, his appetites sometimes overcame him: "There have been times when overeating has stolen upon your servant. By your mercy may you keep it far from me!")

But the same "unholy curiosity" that led Augustine toward the pleasures of this world also pushed him toward a search for Light and Truth.
For years he was a devotee of a vegetarian cult called the Manichees,
which pictured primal forces of good and evil as forever at war, and left
room only for a vestigial Christianity. He later grew sympathetic to the
Skeptics, who held that one could be sure of nothing.

The ascetic side of Augustine warred with the hedonistic. Modern
psychiatrists might be quick to see them as but two sides of a single coin
—an extremist personality at odds with itself. Nonetheless, this clash of
temperaments launched a soul-searching that, through the *Confessions*,
still impresses with its insight and sincerity.

Swayed by intellectual and spiritual factors, but also plainly moved
by the piety of his mother (who would later herself be canonized),
Augustine was ultimately won over to the Church. The scene in the
garden in which he finally breaks into anguished tears before his Lord is
particularly moving. But even more so is the death of his mother: After
she dies, Augustine writes, "I closed her eyes, and a great wave of sorrow
surged into my heart...It was because I was now bereft of all the comfort
that I had had from her that my soul was wounded and my life seemed
shattered, for her life and mine had been as one."

One need hardly embrace the Catholic faith to find the story of
Augustine's search for higher truth uplifting—or, for that matter, to find
the battle between his warring selves dramatic. For all of us with personal
demons to exorcise or faced with a choice between the high road and the
low, Augustine offers a lofty model.

"The eye is attracted by beautiful objects, by gold and silver and all
such things. There is great pleasure, too, in feeling something agreeable
to the touch, and material things have various qualities to please each of
the other senses." Yet one follows the path of sin, Augustine tells God,
"when one love[s] the things you have created instead of loving you." ❖

# The Golem

By Gustav Meyrink
First published in 1915

The stark terror of a Poe mystery and the existential torment of an early Ingmar Bergman film grafted onto an Isaac Bashevis Singer story: That, in crude outline, is *The Golem*, by Gustav Meyrink.

"Once in every generation a spiritual disturbance zigzags, like a flash of lightning, right through the Ghetto, taking possession of the souls of the living to some end we know not of, and rising in the form of a wraith that appears to our senses in the guise of a human entity." This, as Meyrink relates the legend through a minor character's monologue, is the Golem, an early Jewish predecessor of Frankenstein's monster. Every thirty-three years, according to folklore, it roams the crowded alleys of the Prague ghetto, leaving terror and confusion in its wake.

Yet as befits a being first given human form, according to legend, by a sixteenth-century rabbi, the Golem has another, more spiritual side. This slant-eyed creature, half human and half supernatural, confronts those it meets with the alien elements of their own personalities, provoking in them spiritual crisis. And that is the fate that befalls the protagonist of Meyrink's bizarre tale, Athanasius Pernath.

Pernath, we learn, is a gem cutter whose past mental breakdown has left him with a great empty hole in the center of his memory. Now, in the days of the Golem's return to Prague, the aching mystery of his own past threatens his composure. He dreams obsessively of a stone that is like a lump of fat. The Golem gives him a book whose words come to life as he reads them: "From an invisible mouth words were streaming forth, turning into living entities, and winging straight towards me. They twirled and paraded like gaily dressed female slaves, only to sink on the floor or evaporate in iridescent mist." Later, from the jail cell in which he is incarcerated for suspected murder, Pernath looks out to see a clock face without hands.

The whole novel is like that, a succession of dreams, reveries and horrors punctuated by intervals of waking consciousness. Soon, the line between what's real and what's not blurs. The reader first struggles to maintain the distinction. But ultimately, he's swept along on the tide of Meyrink's imagination, and the line breaks down altogether. The sensation is freeing.

To be sure, conventional plot elements coexist with the fantastic. A villainous junk dealer, Aaron Wassertrum, wishes to reveal an affair between one Dr. Savioli and a local countess. The sly, scheming Charousek, meanwhile, seeks revenge on Wassertrum. Hillel, knowledgeable of Kabbala, the body of mystic Jewish belief, gives Pernath spiritual sustenance. We encounter hidden letters, clandestine meetings, crowded evenings spent at Loisitschek's, the local haunt for neighborhood lowlifes ...Most of these more realistic scenes are set in the dark rooms, lightless alleys and gloomy stairways and passages of the Prague ghetto. Yet they are like the clear light of day compared to Pernath's encounters with the Golem and his own hidden past—truly, dark nights of the soul.

At least by one translation from the German, Meyrink's novel is sometimes choppy, its dialogue archaic, its pages cluttered with exclamation points and other typographical devices, its story unnecessarily twisted back on itself. Still, the ambience created is haunting. One senses a gifted amateur at work, a writer of extraordinary gifts who has yet to refine his craft. Indeed, *The Golem* was Meyrink's first novel, and appeared when he was forty-seven, after an already full life spent as banker, champion athlete, occultist, prison inmate (three months for embezzlement), and finally short story writer and editor.

He died in 1932. A few years later *The Golem* and the other works of Gustav Meyrink were among the first to be burned by the Nazis. ❖

# The Razor's Edge

*By W. Somerset Maugham*
*First published in 1944*

The settings are exotic, the characters memorable, the story believable. But what most stays with you about W. Somerset Maugham's *The Razor's Edge* is the curious way in which the main character inhabits the distant periphery of the novel, not its center.

Early on, Maugham's lengthy and affectionate description of Elliott Templeton places this art dealer, rake, and connoisseur of decadence at stage center. Only imperceptibly does one realize that no, it's not Elliott but Larry Darrell—"a pleasant-looking boy, neither handsome nor plain, rather shy and in no way remarkable"—who is the main character. We normally see Elliott up close, while Larry remains shadowy, and this inversion of foreground and background runs all through the novel, haunting it.

The story takes place in the years after World War I. Larry, a veteran of aerial dogfights over Europe in which he was almost killed, has just returned to Chicago. He is a changed man. While his friends hurry back to promising careers, he seems bent on a mysterious personal quest. He won't talk about his war experiences. He spends hour upon hour in the library reading, studying, thinking.

At first it seems he may yet marry Isabel, the charming but willful daughter of Elliott Templeton's sister. There's only one hitch. He has no job, and shows no inclination to get one. Rather, he's perfectly willing to live on his meager trust fund. He wants to "loaf," he tells Isabel, by which he means to study, travel and experience the world. She declines his offer of marriage, and instead marries Gray Maturin, the solid, resolutely conventional, cliche-bound son of an investment broker.

Years pass. The stock market crashes, sweeping away the Maturin fortune (though Gray manages to keep Isabel in Dior dresses). The action shifts to Paris and to the Riviera. Larry is rarely seen. At one point, he takes up with a childhood friend from Chicago, with whom he used to read poetry, but who has now descended to a life of drunkenness and wanton sensuality. Ultimately, he travels to India and meets a guru, Shri Ganesha.

The narrator of these events is pictured as far removed from them. He learns what happens, often years later, only through long conversations with the principals. The reader, in turn, learns of them third-hand, and then only when the narrator sees fit to tell us. It is a curious device. But it works: the mystery deepens, the alpine mist envelops Larry, and his life thickens.

In the book's opening pages, the narrator apologizes for calling it a novel, insisting that all the events and characters are real. Indeed, the narrator bears the name of Maugham, who wrote a novel called *The Moon and Sixpence*, which the real Maugham did write. No doubt the biographers can say whether the author's apology is just a literary device or, on the other hand, means that Larry, Isabel and Elliott really lived.

But it hardly matters. Fiction or fact, *The Razor's Edge* illuminates the conflict between the pull of the spirit and the pleasures of home, family, work and social life. Maugham sympathizes—a little too unambivalently for my taste—with Larry's spiritual side. Indeed, in a whodunit-like twist, Isabel stoops to a contemptible and destructive act that casts all she represents of the earth-bound and the conventional in the blackest light.

Eventually, Larry gives up his slim inheritance and plans to return to the United States, to bring some of the wisdom of the East to his spirit-starved homeland. This he will accomplish, he tells Maugham, by buying a taxi cab, which will give him both the mobility and livelihood he needs. In America, he explains, "it would be an equivalent to the staff and the begging-bowl of the wandering mendicant."

Since that conversation, the narrator tells us, he has heard nothing of Larry. But "I have never since taken a taxi, in New York, without glancing up on the chance that I might meet Larry's gravely smiling, deep-set eyes."

Many readers of *The Razor's Edge* will find themselves looking for him, too. ❖

# The Seven Storey Mountain

*By Thomas Merton*
*First published in 1948*

In the final pages of *The Seven Storey Mountain*, Thomas Merton, a Trappist monk living in the Cistercian monastery of Our Lady of Gethsemani in Kentucky, complains to God: "You have contradicted everything. You have left me in no-man's land." For while now at last committed to solitude and the contemplative life, he is still being urged by the abbot to write poems, books, even essays and magazine articles, for the world down below.

Son of an accomplished English painter and his American wife, a former student at Cambridge and Columbia Universities, well-trained in the ways of intellectual and literary life in the secular world, Merton, it seems, has a double vocation. And his need to express his thoughts on paper interferes with his hard-won new life as a white-robed member of the order. "There was this shadow, this double, this writer who had followed me into the cloister," he writes, leaving him in bondage to "contracts, reviews, page proofs and all the plans for books and articles that I am saddled with."

Though the conflict surfaces only late in the book, there are whispers of it all along. *The Seven Storey Mountain* is, first of all, a spiritual autobiography, full of Merton's crises of faith and doubts about his true vocation, and finally his slow, winding journey up to Gethsemani. He recounts his early travels with his father in the monastery-studded French countryside, his days at boarding school and in the university, his adolescent insecurities, his flirtations with communism, his disillusionment with the clamorous world of striving and success, and his conversion to Catholicism.

But always in the background, though never much credited, is Merton as a serious student of literature and philosophy. Indeed, most of his friends are novelists, poets or other literary types, and he himself teaches literature and writes.

The chasm between his two halves is enormous, perhaps greater than even Merton realizes. In one paragraph he can rhapsodize about Mary, Our Lady, Mother of God, seemingly lost in clouds of what the less spiritually inclined might write off as so much hocus-pocus. And then in the next paragraph, he'll land solidly back on earth, every trace of religiosity extinguished, bringing to life some mundane human experience, often quite sardonically.

Take his depiction of radical chic, circa 1936, at a party held in a Park Avenue apartment of a Barnard College student and Young Communist League member. "There was a big grand piano on which someone played Beethoven while the Reds sat around on the floor. Later we had a sort of Boy Scout campfire group in the living room, singing heavy Communist songs, including that delicate anti-religious classic, 'There'll be a Pie in the Sky when you Die.' "

Or consider how he describes English sentimentality as a "big, vague, sweet complex of subjective dispositions regarding the English countryside...games of cricket in the long summer afternoon...and all those other things the mere thought of which produces a kind of warm and inexpressible ache in the English heart."

This is someone who, six years after joining the monastery, can admit: "Is there any man who has ever gone through a whole lifetime without dressing himself up, in his fancy, in the habit of a monk and enclosing himself in a cell where he sits magnificent in heroic austerity and solitude, while all the young ladies who hitherto were cool to his affections in the world come and beat on the gates of the monastery crying, 'Come out, come out!' " Merton, it seems to me, acts more surprised than he has any right to be when he complains that the writer that is his other half "meets me in the doorway of all my prayers, and follows me into church. He kneels with me behind the pillar, the Judas, and talks to me all the time in my ear."

Still, he did it: At the age of twenty-six, he became a monk. And he lived that way until his death, at the age of fifty-three. Few readers will be so moved by Merton's example that they're ready to follow him into the cloister; most will not share his faith, much less his devotion. Still, there is much here for them, too. For while Merton climbs the mountains, he tells us much about the valley below in which the rest of us reside.

"We live in a society," he writes, "whose whole policy is to excite every nerve in the human body and keep it at the highest pitch of artificial tension, to strain every human desire to the limit and to create as many new desires and synthetic passions as possible."

A degree of serenity awaits us, Merton's life suggests, if we can but shut up long enough, cease our striving long enough, to listen and to see. ❖

# Death Be Not Proud

*By John Gunther*
*First published in 1949*

"He had the most brilliant promise of any child I have ever known," one of his doctors said after he died. He played the recorder, collected stamps, sailed, and rode horses. He performed chemistry experiments, studied Einstein's theory of relativity. He was genuinely kind and good; even as a teenager, he was protective of others' feelings. He displayed high intelligence and lively wit. Once, asked what he wanted to eat when at last freed from the medically prescribed diet on which he'd been placed, he replied: "A glass of full milk, an artichoke with hollandaise sauce, spaghetti and meatballs and a chocolate ice-cream soda."

His name was John Gunther, namesake of his father, the best-selling author of *Inside Europe* and its successors. He would have been seventy at century's end, but he died at age seventeen, of a brain tumor, in 1947. *Death Be Not Proud*—the title comes from a poem by John Donne—is his father's memoir of the final fifteen months of his life.

During that period, his parents sought treatment or cure in specialist after specialist. They tried surgery, x-rays, a peculiar mustard treatment, and a controversial low-salt, low-sugar, low-protein diet that for a while seemed to arrest the tumor. Sometimes, Johnny seemed to get better; once or twice, he improved so dramatically they were left jubilant at the prospect of cure. But always the tumor returned—though never, up until the day he died, did it undermine his intellect. Only the worsening left side of his body hinted at the eruption in the right occipital lobe of his brain.

His parents consulted thirty-two or thirty-three physicians by the time Johnny died. The author hints that this ran into a lot of money, and that he was in debt, but in the end Johnny benefited from almost limitless medical resources, including some of the foremost specialists in the United States and Canada. Access to medical care in this country, we're reminded, is not now, and never has been democratic. Yet even the finest medical care is sometimes powerless to defy nature's will.

Though a story of one boy's illness and death, *Death Be Not Proud* also grants insight into a remarkable family and a rarefied world. There is, of course, the author himself, a globe-trotting figure who inhabits an elegant Park Avenue world of maids and fine restaurants in the years before New York became so difficult; who counts among his friends famous publishers and authors; whose report on the day's activities is apt to include mention of a Book-of-the-Month Club sale.

Then there is Johnny, the dying prodigy, who comes alive not alone through the filter of his father's perceptions but through his own letters to parents, teachers and friends, and through diary entries. If death is made more tragic in proportion to the nobility of the life it extinguishes, Johnny's is a great tragedy.

Finally, there is Frances Gunther, the author's divorced wife, who during Johnny's illness moves from her house in the country to John's Manhattan apartment, while John camps out at a nearby hotel. Even from John Gunther's account it's plain that mother and son shared a special relationship, that Johnny could talk to her as he probably couldn't to his father, that for the two of them Jesus and Buddha, truth and goodness, lived.

In a brief final chapter, we encounter Frances in her own words, close up. If John Gunther is all journalistic restraint, Frances is all poetry, passion and lofty ideals. "I was trying to create of him a newer kind of human being: an aware person, without fear, and with love: a sound individual, adequate of life anywhere on earth, and loving life everywhere and always. We would talk about this as our experiment together."

So *Death Be Not Proud* is not just the clinical record of the doctors' failure to restore a sick boy to health. It is a report on a great experiment in which the stream of vibrant "data" that was Johnny's personality and intellect sadly, prematurely, stopped. ❖

# *Ecclesiastes*

*From the Old Testament*

The work of literature that is *Ecclesiastes* has blessed our culture with at least two book titles—Ernest Hemingway's *The Sun Also Rises*, and *Earth Abides* by George R. Stewart. Quotation compendiums abound with its poetic riches. The words of a popular song from the 1960s, "Turn, Turn, Turn," are taken directly from what is perhaps its most lyrical passage, beginning: "To every thing there is a season, and a time to every purpose under the heaven..."

"Koheleth," its would-be author, is actually a transliteration from Hebrew of a word that in Greek became "Ecclesiastes," and which means a preacher who addresses a public assembly. Though traditionally ascribed to King Solomon, who lived in the tenth century B.C., Ecclesiastes almost certainly dates from much later, perhaps as late as 200 B.C.

Apparently admitted to full scriptural standing only in 100 A.D. at the Synod of Jamnia, Ecclesiastes has been termed "the most heretical book of the third century B.C." Heretical, perhaps, in that there's so little explicitly religious about it. Indeed, some scholars see, in certain almost formulaic references to God, the hand of a pious post-Koheleth figure who sought to make it more explicitly God-fearing.

*Ecclesiastes'* spiritual content would seem to bear as much kinship to the Eastern philosophical tradition, with its stress on the futility of worldly desires, as to orthodox Judaism or traditional Christianity. It worries more about this life than the next. Even as it emphasizes the inevitability of death, it extols the ordinary pleasures of daily living.

Indeed, it invests with a cloak of wisdom what many do quite naturally: "Enjoy life with the wife whom thou lovest all the days of thy vanity;

for that is thy portion in life, and in thy labour where thou labourest under the sun. Whatsoever thy hand attaineth to do by thy strength, that do; for there is no work, nor device, nor knowledge, nor wisdom, in the grave, whither thou goest."

Its recurring admonition, "all is vanity and striving after wind," is delivered with the relentlessness of a meditational mantra. Or perhaps, with the same power with which modern advertising drives home a single, simple message over and over again, embellished from time to time, but in the end always the same: *Life is short. All our strivings are for nothing. Death awaits us all.*

Pessimistic? In a sense. One's hopes and dreams, one's labors, one's accumulations of knowledge or wealth—all amount to but a "striving after wind."

Yet the idea is freeing, too. For in dashing prospects of some Grand Theme to life, *Ecclesiastes* enriches *little* themes—marriage, children, work. *Eat, drink and be merry?* Why, you heard it first in *Ecclesiastes*: "So I commend mirth," writes Koheleth, "that a man hath no better thing under the sun, than to eat, and to drink, and to be merry, and that this should accompany him in his labour all the days of his life which God hath given him."

So there's something oddly comforting about the seemingly grim message of *Ecclesiastes*: While humankind's daily struggle may count for nothing in the end,

> *The earth abideth forever.*
> *The sun also ariseth, and the sun goeth down,*
> *And hastest to his place where he ariseth,*
> *The wind goeth toward the south,*
> *And turneth unto the north;*
> *It turneth about continually in its circuit.*
>
> ...

*That which hath been is that which shall be,*
*And that which hath been done is that which shall be done;*
*And there is nothing new under the heavens.*

Churchgoers, and their non-Christian counterparts, often need little prompting to dip into their Old or New Testaments. But non-believers today—it was not so true in years past—will sometimes read everything in sight before turning to the Bible, choosing to spurn the conventional wisdom that sees in it much wisdom and beauty.

*Ecclesiastes* proves the conventional wisdom right. "It was a wise providence," an interpreter has written of Koheleth, "that gave this man's work a place in scripture." ❖

# Lost Horizon

*By James Hilton*
*First published in 1933*

Half a century ago, with publication of James Hilton's *Lost Horizon*, a new word began its absorption into the English language. *Shangri-La*, says the dictionary today, means "an imaginary, remote paradise on earth." Hilton pictures a far-off world (yet here, on our planet), peopled with "aliens" endowed with mysterious powers (yet who look just like us). The effect is that of science fiction, only without the science.

*Lost Horizon* is set in the Far East, following one of the native revolts that periodically rocked Britain's colonial empire. Four Westerners are being airlifted out of pillaged Baskul, India, when one of them, glimpsing the pilot, becomes suspicious. Later, he looks out the window and instead of seeing spread beneath him the airport at Peshawar, their destination, sees "an opaque mist, veiling an immense, sun-brown desolation." Later comes a bared revolver, an unscheduled landing and refueling, renewed flight...

Ultimately, they crash in a valley hidden high in Tibet, icy mountain peaks of unspeakable beauty rising around them. The pilot dies, and they are left, alone, huddled against howling winds. Soon they meet a group of stocky Tibetans in sheepskins bearing an elderly Chinese in a sedan chair, Chang, whose impeccable English is laced with Shakespeare. Chang and the Tibetans escort the four of them across the valley to the lamasery known as Shangri-La.

A benign theocracy of lamas, most of them versed in music, literature, and the arts, Shangri-La reveres moderation above all. "We rule with moderate strictness," Chang tells them, "and in return we are satisfied with moderate obedience. And I think I can claim that our people are moderately sober, moderately chaste, and moderately honest."

Of the four Westerners the author brings to Shangri-La, three qualify as little more than stock characters. There's Miss Brinklow, the missionary worker, single-minded in her faith and oozing disdain for "native" ways. And Barnard, a plain-talking American apparently on oil company business, his speech littered with "I reckons" and "gees." And young, pink-cheeked Mallinson—blunt, impetuous, lacking in grace, impatient with Eastern impassivity.

The best developed of the four is Conway, a former Oxford don and now an officer in Britain's consular service. One foot in the world of action and power, the other in that of quiet and contemplation, Conway has just helped negotiate the safe release of eighty Westerners from Baskul—an act exciting young Mallinson's admiration. Yet now, in Shangri-La, the other side of Conway's personality emerges. Relaxed about their predicament, he actually seems to enjoy his luxurious captivity. Mallinson is incensed. Why doesn't Conway want to leave this crazy, godforsaken place?

For a reader buffeted by the storms of modern life, it hardly seems surprising. Sheltered from the wind and isolated from the cares of the world, Shangri-La looks down upon a verdant valley, up to towering, mountain peaks. Its library is stocked with the finest literature of both West and East. Its moderation-in-all-things ethic extends even to sex. The food is well prepared, Chang's conversation always lively, the bathing facilities luxurious.

Indeed, presumably stuck there for only two months—after which time an expedition from the outside was to presumably guide them back out—three of the four travelers sink comfortably into their new lives, reluctant to leave, ever. Mallinson, alone among them, does not. His nervous hankering to be gone from the place never diminishes. "There's something dark and evil about it," he says of Shangri-La.

And though that sentiment comes from the least attractive of the characters—one easy to write off as inflexible, immature, and mired in the trivialities of the world outside—the reader's feelings about Shangri-La take a subtle turn. As do, for that matter, Conway's, whose private conversations with the High Lama have revealed to him many of Shangri-La's mysteries.

In all the subsequent action, that fleeting doubt is never erased. Is there something ugly and unnatural in life up here, away from the cares of the world? And is there something noble and good, after all, in Western striving? Those haunting questions make *Lost Horizon* more provocative by far than the one-dimensional Message novel it might otherwise have become. ❖

# Bhagavad Gita *("Song of God")*

*Sanskrit poem probably written between 500 and 200 B.C.*

For what is held up as one of Hinduism's most sacred texts, it begins inauspiciously enough. The warrior Arjuna stands upon the field of battle, on the eve of the fighting. He is stricken with fear, disconsolate at the prospect of the many lives sure to be lost, many from his family. "Life goes from my limbs," he wails, "and my mouth is sear and dry; a trembling overcomes my body, and my hair shudders in horror."

Whereupon the deity Krishna asks: "Whence this lifeless dejection, Arjuna, in this hour, the hour of trial? Strong men know not despair, Arjuna, for this wins neither heaven nor earth. Fall not into degrading weakness, for this becomes not a man who is a man."

Is this how the *Bhagavad Gita* reveals the great Krishna, god of the Hindus? As a macho god who, far from urging peace and reconciliation, encourages the coming slaughter?

Even Arjuna is bothered: "Why does thou enjoin upon me the terrible action of war? My mind is in confusion because in thy words I find contradictions."

But Krishna is no god of war. Something else is going on here, something alien to western sensibilities. For Krishna is saying, It doesn't matter. Do not hold out against the inevitable battle. Do not rail at events. Do not strive to overturn them. "Action is greater than inaction; perform therefore thy task in life."

The battle will be terrible? Men will die? Arjuna may die? None of this matters, counsels Krishna. "Weapons cannot hurt the Spirit and fire can never burn him. Untouched is he by drenching waters, untouched is he by parching winds." Life and death are but worldly preoccupations. The body does not count, the senses are an illusion. "From the world of the senses, Arjuna, comes heat and comes cold, and pleasure and pain. They come and they go; they are transient. Arise above them, strong soul." Spirit is all.

Employing surprisingly linear, almost "scientific" logic, Krishna outlines just how worldly strivings lead to sorrow: "When a man dwells on the pleasures of sense, attraction for them arises in him. From attraction arises desire, the lust of possession, and this leads to passion, anger," ultimately to confusion of mind, loss of reason, destruction.

For Krishna, the ascetic diet, the sexual orgy, working too hard or working not at all, all equally reflect disharmony. "A harmony in eating and resting, in sleeping and keeping awake; a perfection in whatever one does. This is the Yoga that gives peace from all pain." Balance, evenness, calm.

The visible world around us, says Krishna, is illusion. Distinctions meaningful to us—light and darkness, beginnings and ends—all are but manifestations of the same One. "I am the cleverness of the gambler's dice," says Krishna. "I am the beauty of all things beautiful. I am victory and the struggle for victory. I am the goodness of those who are good." All is but a single radiance. Victory and defeat. Life and death. Why strive for one or the other?

"He who feels neither excitement nor repulsion, who complains not and lusts not for things; who is beyond good and evil, and who has love —he is dear to me," says Krishna.

Echoes can be heard here of, for example, the New Testament; but mostly all this stands wildly distant from the Western emphasis on achievement, expression, energy bent on changing the world, and out of which came Picasso, Einstein and Freud.

"To strive, to seek, to find, and not to yield," urges Tennyson in "Ulysses." Everything in the *Bhagavad Gita* argues to the contrary. To cease striving. To seek no more. To yield.

Can the two outlooks be reconciled?

Hardly. Our turbulent inner lives tell of the eternal war between them. ❖

# Night

*By Elie Wiesel*
*First published in 1958*

That there should be such a genre as "Holocaust literature" is itself a tragedy. So terrible was the murder and madness of the Nazis, on so great a scale their destruction of European Jewry and others, so threatening to faith the enormity of their crimes, that thousands of scholars, journalists and holocaust survivors have struggled to make sense of it. One of the first to do so, in *Night*, was Elie Wiesel, a Romanian Jew who survived the Auschwitz and Buchenwald concentration camps, and who saw most of the residents of his little Transylvanian town, Sighet, including his mother, father, and sister, murdered.

His story starts innocently enough, as a poor man with great, dreaming eyes teaches thirteen-year-old Wiesel cabbala, Judaism's mystical tradition. "Then one day they expelled all the foreign Jews from Sighet." His teacher was one of them. "What can we expect?" says a townsman. "It's war..." Nothing out of the ordinary.

Life returns to normal. It is 1942. Outside, in the air over Germany, on the outskirts of Stalingrad, war rages. But in Sighet, all is as it has been. "I continued to devote myself to my studies. By day, the Talmud, at night, the cabbala. My father was occupied with his business and the doings of the community. My grandfather had come to celebrate the New Year with us, so that he could attend the services of the famous rabbi of Borsche. My mother began to think that it was high time to find a suitable young man for Hilda."

Suddenly, German soldiers appear. One officer takes up residence in the Kahn house, just across from Wiesel's home. "They said he was a charming man—calm, likable, polite and sympathetic. Three days after he moved in he brought Madame Kahn a box of chocolates."

On the seventh day of Passover, the leaders of the Jewish community are arrested. "From that moment, everything happened very quickly. The race toward death had begun."

*The race toward death had begun.*

More artful writers might have avoided such language. Show, don't tell, says good writing practice. Don't destroy hard-won immediacy with flights of melodrama. This is not the only time Wiesel evinces such a superficial lack of literary polish.

Yet, peculiarly, what might otherwise be a defect here enhances the author's credibility. It is as if *Night* had been not so much "composed" as plucked whole from a ravaged heart. His is no mere pretty rendering, Wiesel seems to tell us. The horrors he experienced fall beyond the rules and restraints of "art." Giving vent to his grief, anger and despair comes first. He must throw in his lot with his town and his people, not with the worldwide community of literati.

The story unfolds...

The order comes down that the Jews of Sighet must henceforth wear a yellow star.

Barbed wire goes up around the town, now a true ghetto. The houses forming its perimeter have any windows that face the street boarded shut.

The ghetto's inhabitants learn they are to be deported. They wait.

Finally, they are herded into cattle cars so tightly that they can sit only by taking turns. All during the trip, a madwoman, broken by her separation from her husband and sons, consumed by visions of fire and flame, howls out her despair. Then, days later, as the train pulls up to the concentration camp gates, her vision comes true. "Suddenly, our doors opened...In front of us flames. In the air, that smell of burning flesh. It must have been midnight. We had arrived—at Birkenau, reception center for Auschwitz."

A reel of black-and-white film documentary from the Nuremberg becomes one young man's life. At the end, having been moved to Buchenwald and liberated by the Americans, Wiesel views himself in a mirror for the first time since leaving Sighet. "From the depths of the mirror, a corpse gazed back at me. The look in his eyes, as they stared into mine, has never left me." ❖

# The Varieties of Religious Experience

By William James
First published in 1902

This classic is about what some people experience in quiet moments when God reaches out and touches them.

Do not, atheist or skeptic, thereby dismiss it as so much religious mumbo-jumbo. Do not, Sunday church-goer, presume that you'll find your Lord's divinity affirmed.

*The Varieties of Religious Experience* has nothing to say about churches, priests and solemn ritual. It is about personal religious experience as reported by some of the great spiritual figures of history, from Loyola and Martin Luther to St. Teresa and Walt Whitman.

Born-again Christians, cultists, ascetics from the Middle Ages who sleep on nails, all the way to those expressing the most sublime spiritual sensibilities—these are the subject of James's brilliant work. It dissects their experiences, maps how those destined for religious fulfillment find it. And though steeped in the Western scientific tradition, it is apt to leave even skeptics convinced there's something outside everyday experience every bit as real and true as the shattering of a glass or the smell of a rose.

Concludes James, in the final chapter, after four hundred pages of impressive tentativeness: "The whole drift of my education goes to persuade me that the world of our present consciousness is only one out of many worlds of consciousness that exist, and that those other worlds must contain experiences which have a meaning for our life also; and that although in the main their experiences and those of this world keep discreet, yet the two become continuous at certain points, and higher energies filter in."

James's book is the product of a twenty-lecture series he gave at the

University of Edinburgh around the turn of the century. A philosopher and psychologist, the father of the school of philosophy known as pragmatism, and a giant of his time of the stature of Freud, James described his approach to his subject as psychological. He called his first lecture "Religion and Neurology," and even sometimes applied the capital "S" to "Subjects" whose conversions and trances he described, in the style of a psychological report. Sometimes he exhibits almost boyish enthusiasm as one of his subjects displays what strikes him as particularly "interesting" behavior.

These lectures argue forcibly that religion need not be valued only on the basis of the truths it presumes to reveal, but in its impact on believers; that, quite aside from the truth of its teachings, religion has value in the personal experiences it bestows. The monk comes away moved by his vision of God, and comforted by his knowledge of Him. The alcoholic, feeling a higher Presence beside him, gives up his whiskey and devotes his life to more productive ends. Dare science, or a too-small spirit, negate or deny these? The experiences themselves, says James, are facts—as crisp and real as the wind blowing across your cheek.

For James, displaying a suppleness of mind that leaves him untroubled by seeming opposites, the scientific and the spiritual stand side by side. In a chapter called "The Reality of the Unseen," he advances the kind of argument heard more often these days from the hard sciences—that any theory is but a model, a creation of the mind, a pretty picture that only inadequately describes a portion of the Universe, and that the Universe exists quite apart from man's efforts to describe it. If we believe something, James says, it is real to us. The "articulately verbalized philosophy" we build around it is "but its showy translation into formulas ...Instinct leads, intelligence does but follow."

Whenever it is James himself who speaks, the book seems to fairly shine. Which, owing to many pages of others' testimony about various religious experiences, is not always. Displaying just that striking consistency the author is at pains to highlight, these sometimes grow wearisome. So when James reappears with some impeccably formulated interpretation of all we've read, we greet him eagerly.

What a delight to hear him speak! In no book I've recently read has the visual phenomenon we call "brilliance" felt so acutely alive in words. I offer no brief examples of this, because this is not a brilliance that reveals itself in snippets of felicitous expression but rather what emerges in whole, lengthy paragraphs that read like multifaceted diamonds, sparkling in the sun. They do not inspire the reader, or move him, so much as leave him breathless at the working of a great mind.

You feel that James sits beside you in a room, with just you alone, anticipating your objections, speaking to your doubts, sharing your excitement—finally grasping your hand for an intellectual and spiritual voyage that leaves you gasping with the sheer pleasure of "Ah, yes, yes, of course." ❖

# Acknowledgments

I owe thanks to many. First, to my various editors at the Baltimore *Sun* and *Evening Sun*, where most of these essays first appeared, especially to Gwinn Owens, who shepherded them into print over the longest span of years, and to Mike Bowler; as well as to the late Art Seidenbaum of the *Los Angeles Times*.

To the whole crew at Bancroft Press who helped bring this book into being, in particular publisher Bruce Bortz who saw in these essays, gathered together, something like the book I saw in them; special thanks to Bancroft's Sarah Azizi for her invaluable, consistently intelligent editorial help.

To Vicky Bijur, for her fortitude and good sense.

To my son David, for his help from the outset, especially with *Kim*, G. H. Hardy, and Isadora Duncan.

And to Judy, my wife of sixteen years, whom I met just about the time I conceived of "Vintage Reading"; it was a very good year.

Most of all, thanks to my mother, Beatrice Kanigel, whose own love of literature spilled over onto me and made me first want to read books, and then to write them.